Social Media Recruitment

How to successfully integrate social media into recruitment strategy

Andy Headworth

KoganPage

LONDON   PHILADELPHIA   NEW DELHI

First published in Great Britain and the United States in 2015 by Kogan Page Limited

2nd Floor, 45 Gee Street	1518 Walnut Street, Suite 1100	4737/23 Ansari Road
London EC1V 3RS	Philadelphia PA 19102	Daryaganj
United Kingdom	USA	New Delhi 110002
www.koganpage.com		India

© Andy Headworth, 2015

The right of Andy Headworth to be identified as the author of this work has been asserted by him in accordance with the Copyright, Designs and Patents Act 1988.

ISBN   978 0 7494 7370 9
E-ISBN   978 0 7494 7371 6

British Library Cataloguing-in-Publication Data

A CIP record for this book is available from the British Library.

Library of Congress Cataloging-in-Publication Data
Headworth, Andy.
  Social media recruitment : how to successfully integrate social media into recruitment strategy / Andy Headworth.
    pages cm
    ISBN 978-0-7494-7370-9 (paperback) – ISBN 978-0-7494-7371-6 (ebk)   1. Employees–Recruiting.
2. Social media.   3. Personnel management.   I. Title.
    HF5549.5.R44H43 2015
    658.3'11102854678–dc23
                                                                                2015008795

Typeset by Graphicraft Limited, Hong Kong
Print production managed by Jellyfish
Printed and bound by CPI Group (UK) Ltd, Croydon, CR0 4YY

PRAISE FOR
SOCIAL MEDIA
RECRUITMENT

'This well-written definitive guide to social media recruitment is an essential resource for integrating social media into recruitment strategies and processes. The book's comprehensive and practical approach, with compelling case studies, provides a strategic framework and a clear road map, all in an insightful and engaging way.'
Heather Travis, Director, Asia Pacific, Armstrong Craven, and Chairman, Executive Research Association (ERA)

'With social recruiting, there is no one silver bullet or strategy. *Social Media Recruitment* is one of the most comprehensive sources for all things social media recruiting to date.'
Jessica Miller-Merrell, Founder of Blogging4Jobs

'This book is a must-read for recruiters, entrepreneurs, leaders and managers. Why? Because it helps them overcome the fear and doubts they have regarding using social media for recruitment and is a great, veracious guide to successfully doing that.'
René Bolier, Co-Founder, OnRecruit

'Andy is the social media and recruitment expert that the experts in the industry seek out to read and listen to. His advice is spot on and supported by years of diverse consulting experience. After seven years in the social media recruitment arena, you'd think I'd know it all. Andy's book is chock-full of case studies that are inspiring for my firm and clients. For years I've made Andy's a blog a weekly must-read. His book surpasses his blog, with detailed case studies and examples of how to use social media properly to recruit.'
Kelly Dingee, Director, Strategic Recruiting at Staffing Advisors

'Andy's blog has been a must-read for me over the last several years. His clear writing style helps recruiters sharpen their social media skills. With this book I hope recruiters, who are still not social media savvy, will build their skills and be relevant in a changing business world.'
Gautam Ghosh, Director, Talent Branding, Flipkart.com, and Blogger at http://gauteg.blogspot.com

'To me, Andy Headworth is the world's pre-eminent authority in the area of social recruiting. His blogs on the ongoing process of using social media to recruit are always spot on and serve as a text book for best practices in social recruiting. I learn something valuable in every post, every blog, and every comment.'
Brenda Burch, Chief Retail Talent Sourcer, Bjork Enterprises Ltd

'Any recruiting leader wanting to up their game in social recruiting will want to read this from cover to cover.'
Tony Restell, Founder, Social-Hire.com

'The definitive guide to social media recruitment. Packed with practical advice and examples, this book makes a compelling case for social recruiting for even the most hardened social media sceptic. A must-read for those new to social recruiting, but with plenty of great content for those who are already social too.'
Gemma Reucroft, HR Director, Tunstall Group

'Having worked in Recruitment/Talent Acquisition for 20 odd years, the current environment is exciting, fast paced, quickly evolving and for many ...scary. Andy gets this, and this book is really going to help you. The vital importance of snaring good people is critical to business success. This book will give you the edge to get great people inside your walls.'
Hassanah Rudd, Australia Recruitment Manager, Fletcher Building

'A brilliant business book for anyone looking to successfully integrate social media in their recruitment strategy. Andy's knowledge of recruitment strategy, candidate attraction and content marketing strategy, as well as social media technologies, is unsurpassed and he delivers that knowledge in an interesting and meaningful way.'
Louise Triance, MD, UK Recruiter

'It's not often that you find a resource that not only outlines the current recruitment landscape in a meaningful way, but also gives practical steps for Talent Acquisition leaders to take to improve their results. Andy Headworth accomplishes this. Understanding the critical skill shortages in organizations is a key factor in any recruitment strategy being effective. Andy tackles this with ease and includes case studies to back up all aspects of social media use for recruitment success. Whether you're starting your strategy from the ground up, or you already have a strategy in place, Andy's tips and examples provide direction for leaders on all parts of the spectrum.'
Trish McFarlane, CEO and Co-Founder, HRevolutionize LLP

CONTENTS

ABOUT THE AUTHOR

Andy Headworth has been in the recruitment industry for 25 years, and is still as passionate about recruiting as he was when he first started as a young consultant. He is the founder of Sirona Consulting (**http://sironaconsulting.com**) – a specialist consultancy that helps companies to understand and integrate social media into their recruitment strategies and processes. He is an innovative problem solver who always manages to get you thinking differently about how to solve your recruitment challenges.

Andy's knowledge and expertise has allowed him to successfully deliver projects, workshops and keynote speaking assignments across the UK, Europe, the Middle East, Canada, the United States and Asia-Pacific. In 2013 he was named by The Huffington Post in 'Top 100 Most Social HR Leaders on Twitter' and '50 Most Popular Recruiting Influencers on Twitter' by ERE/LeadTail. He also authors an award-winning blog (**http://sironaconsulting.com/blog**) and recently made a film for the BBC providing social media recruiting guidance. This is Andy's second book, having previously written *Smart Social Media Recruitment Strategies* (2011).

Away from work he enjoys travelling and exploring new countries and cultures, spending time with his wife and children and closely following the fortunes of Liverpool FC.

ACKNOWLEDGEMENTS

It is funny how time mellows your thinking. After writing my first book three years ago, I said I would never write another book again. I learnt much from that experience and writing this second book has been more enjoyable. Thank you to Katy Hamilton at Kogan Page for reaching out to me with the idea for this book initially, I am glad you did.

Writing this book would not have been possible without the support and understanding of Sara, Bethany, Kelly, Joseph, mum and dad during the long hours and lost weekends spent researching and writing. Thank you.

There are a number of people who have been very helpful and without whom many of the examples and stories would have gone untold. So in no particular order I would like to thank the following people for their help, assistance, referrals and content they have provided that have allowed me to write the book I wanted to write: Tim Barry, Dave Martin, Mark Rice, Paul Powell, Marc Mapes, Matt Alder, André Hellström, Paul Jacobs, Peter Gold, Mark Sumner, Chris Russell, Steve Ward, Natasha Collopy, the team at Social Samosa, Shahid Wazed, Amybeth Quinn, Katharine Robinson, Kelly Dingee, Sarang Brahme, Jim Stroud, Oscar Mager, Shannon Pritchett, Martin Lee, Jonathan Campbell, Brett Minchington, Brenda Rigney, Gerry Crispin, Mark Sawyer, Clair Bush, Matthew Ferree, Terry Starr, Pete Kazanjy and Neil Morrison.

Maybe it won't be another three years until the next book.

ACKNOWLEDGMENTS

Introduction

Social media in the workplace can be scary and confusing for many people within human resources (HR) and recruitment, mainly due to a lack of knowledge and understanding of how it works. As you will see in this book, social media has now become mainstream in our everyday life, with thousands of social networks available to everyone across the world. Now, in 2015, it is at the point where there is probably a social network for every facet of our lives. We check them the moment we wake up, via our mobile devices, and we are never far away from all the messages, updates and tweets until we go to bed – we have all become slaves to the digital world around us.

This 'always on' aspect of technology has huge implications for everyone involved in recruitment, including job seekers. Recruitment video technology allows candidates to take interviews when it suits them, mobile technology provides freedom of location and flexibility, and social media gives everyone a voice whenever and wherever they choose to use it. I don't think effective talent acquisition or talent management has ever been harder.

For the last seven years I have been helping companies to understand social media and how best to integrate it into their recruitment strategies and processes. There has been one consistent thread on this journey, and that is that no two companies are the same when it comes to social media. Every single one is different, primarily because social media is people-based and, of course, no two people are alike. Add to that the seemingly unlimited advice, tips, guidelines, success stories, case studies and, of course, horror stories that are prevalent across the internet and it is therefore not surprising when people don't know where to start when deciding to use social media in recruitment.

This book is aimed at small to medium-sized enterprises (SMEs) globally who have social media firmly on their agenda, but as yet have not given it the attention it needs from a recruitment and employer branding perspective. The HR, recruitment and talent leaders of these companies recognize they need to adapt to this ever-changing digital world, but either haven't had the resources available or the knowledge to know where to start. This book has been written in an easy to follow and practical style to deal with this exact problem – to help people in companies who are responsible for hiring talent to better understand social media and how it can be integrated successfully into their day-to-day recruitment activities.

Included in this book are many examples from around the world, showing how companies are using social media in different ways to attract, engage and hire talent. From Twitter competitions in India to augmented reality in New Zealand through to attracting candidates with personalized music playlists in Europe, there are some great innovative recruitment examples to inspire you to get started using social media for your recruitment. I have also reached out to some of the world's best people sourcers, who have kindly shared their extensive knowledge in a chapter wholly dedicated to identifying and sourcing candidates across all the main social networks (Chapter 6).

With talent attraction and retention at the top of the agenda for global business leaders, there is the danger that social media is seen as the magic answer for companies experiencing talent challenges. It isn't. But it is a great addition to existing recruitment processes, methods and technologies.

While there are no rules for using social media in recruitment, there are many examples of companies large and small using social media in innovative ways to reach out to and engage with sought-after talent. There are many examples within this book to help encourage you to think laterally about how your company can use social media in different ways within your recruitment.

Navigating the chapters

The following section gives you a quick walkthrough of the book:

Chapter 1: The fast-changing recruitment landscape looks at the global demand for talent and how it is driving change across companies and specifically within HR and recruitment departments. It covers the business drivers, demographic differences, changing financial climates and the implications for the future growth plans of companies who do not address their future talent needs now.

Chapter 2: Recruitment using social media shows how social media can be used for recruiting to meet the demand for talent. It looks at the scale, reach and depth of social media use around the world, and how this can be tapped into for recruiting purposes. It includes examples of how companies have successfully integrated social media into their recruitment strategies.

Chapter 3: Selecting your social networks examines which social media networks you should consider using for your recruitment and why. It looks at the main social networks and provides best practice guidelines in setting up the networks correctly for use within your recruitment strategy.

Chapter 4: Social media tools covers an extensive number of tools that can be used in all aspects of social media recruitment. They cover social media management, productivity, content creation, monitoring, collaboration and hashtag management.

Chapter 5: Social media recruitment strategy explains what a social media recruitment strategy looks like and how to implement one from the beginning. It breaks down the various aspects of a strategy and provides practical advice on how to manage each of the stages for implementing one at your company.

Chapter 6: Candidate sourcing with social media shows you how to identify and source candidates across all the social networks. It includes detailed advice from some of the world's best sourcers, and provides a wealth of tips, tricks and techniques to discover hard-to-find talent.

Chapter 7: Building your employer brand helps you to understand how to build and develop your employment brand using social media and recruitment content marketing. It will cover identifying your target audience, created and curated content, marketing automation for time efficiencies and multichannel content strategy.

Chapter 8: Social media big data looks at the use of huge volumes of data within recruiting and social media, and how you can use it to make the correct hiring decisions. 'Big data' is a global buzzword and can confuse people, but if you use it correctly it can make the recruiter's job much easier.

Chapter 9: Establishing ROI examines how it is possible to accurately establish a return on investment (ROI) using social media in recruitment. Technology plays a large part in measuring ROI, and I take you through the step-by-step process to establish a tangible ROI using social media for recruiting.

Chapter 10: Social media guidelines offers recommendations of different policies and procedures you should be using when social media is involved in recruiting. It covers employee usage policy, and provides proven examples that you can utilize within your company.

Chapter 11: Building a business case for social media recruitment takes you through the process of how to build a business case for using social media within your recruitment strategy.

Chapter 12: Future recruitment looks at where social media and recruitment may end up and some of the changes that are happening now. Change in HR and recruitment is never as fast as it seems, and it covers technologies including mobile and video interviewing, which your company should already be using as part of its recruitment procedure.

My objective is that when you have finished reading this book you will have learnt that social media is something that can be embraced for recruiting, as opposed to being feared or perceived as a threat. There will be many ways that you will be able to use social media within recruitment at your company, and throughout the book there is practical advice including suggested tools, platforms, hints and tips. The world of social media is huge, and

I make no attempt to cover every area of this vast subject. I have focused on the areas of social media that I believe have a direct impact on recruitment.

What I love about social media in recruitment is that some people are literally just starting off at the beginning while others are at various stages of user maturity. The reality is that with the speed of change within the world of social media, we are all learning new things every day.

Enjoy your journey, and I hope the book helps you to integrate social media successfully into your company's future recruitment.

The fast-changing recruitment landscape

In the last five years we have seen technology improve significantly, economies recover from the financial calamities triggered in 2007, the demographic balance of the workforce change, the proliferation of 'big data' and, of course, we are now very much a social media and mobile world. This has all resulted in the recruiting landscape fundamentally changing for both companies and job seekers.

The last few years have seen global economies move from recessionary to retrenchment and, finally, to investment and growth, which is where we are now in 2015. In this relatively short period of time, the workforce available to sustain this economic growth looks considerably different than it did five years ago.

Through a combination of demographic changes beginning to take effect, advancements in mobile, social and technologies happening quicker than anyone could imagine, educational shortfalls in STEM subjects (science, technology, engineering and mathematics) and the global shift to everything digital, there is now a significant skills shortage across many sectors and industries throughout the world.[1]

A company's ability to find, attract and ultimately recruit skilled talent is going to determine how successful they are in meeting their business growth objectives. Talent acquisition and retention is now firmly on the agenda of chief executive officers (CEOs) and business owners across the world.[2]

So considering the changes we have seen over the past five years, how will you be doing recruiting in the next five years? Many of you will not have even considered this, but the success or failure of your companies could well depend on the strategic recruiting decisions you make in the near future.

Considering the next five years, how are you going to deal with some of the well-documented industry trends that are affecting your recruitment world? Are you even considering them yet? These are a number of the current trends that will need to be addressed within the recruitment functions within companies, if not immediately, then very soon:

- The growing mismatch between the skills that companies need and the talent available: 36 per cent of employers globally reported talent shortages in 2014 according to ManpowerGroup's annual Talent Shortage Survey.
- The shortfall of digital talent: 750,000 additional digitally skilled workers are required in the UK by 2017 in order to capitalize on a £12 billion economic opportunity, according to a report from O2 titled 'The Future Digital Skills Needs of the UK Economy'.
- The changing demographics of multigenerational workforces.
- Recruitment talent within organizations.
- Knowledge gaps as more people with critical skills and knowledge are reaching retirement age, combined with a shortfall of these skills to replace them.
- Fast-changing candidate expectations – behaviours, in-demand and they know it, vocal.
- The extinction of the desktop PC – the move to mobile and tablet.
- Social media recruiting – speed, transparency everywhere.
- Data-based recruiting decision making.

These are not things that you can opt out of, as many of these are impacting talent availability and recruiting right now. While you may not think that these will affect your business, because you have a strong and stable workforce, then think again.

If your employees are that good, they will simply become targets of your competitors who will succeed in attracting them to their company at some stage. With the demand for top talent, there will always be companies looking to offer more to poach good people. Existing employee complacency is as bad as poor recruitment strategy.

How will the current trends in our industry impact your recruitment?

The growing mismatch between the skills companies need and the talent available

This is not a new trend, as there has always been a supply-and-demand rationale behind recruitment. However, the fast-changing technological world of social, mobile, digital and cloud has brought with it requirements for new skills, knowledge and experiences.

This is a global problem and one that can be seen in the data collected by ManpowerGroup in their ninth annual Talent Shortage Survey in 2014 (see Figure 1.1).

FIGURE 1.1   Percentage of employers having difficulty filling jobs

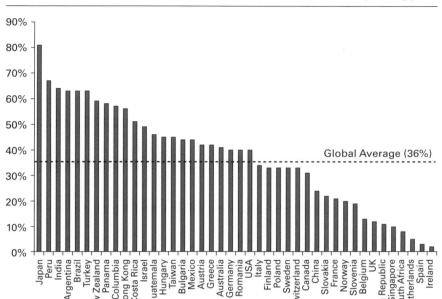

SOURCE: ManpowerGroup Talent Shortage Survey 2014

The global average for talent shortages is 36 per cent, with over half of the countries suffering worse than that. As shown in Figure 1.1 many South American countries are having talent issues. At the other end of the scale, two of the countries that were hit the hardest in the global recession, Spain and Ireland, not unsurprisingly have the lowest talent shortages. How does your country fare, and is your recruitment reflective of this?

If you then combine these talent shortages with the projected gross domestic product (GDP) growth across the world, then you can see in Figure 1.2 that many of the countries face significant challenges in recruiting talent in the foreseeable future.

It is worth noting the types of jobs that global employers are having difficulty filling, because these will impact any recruitment you are planning in the next couple of years. The top 10 jobs causing employers most problems according to ManpowerGroup's survey are:

1 Skilled trade workers.

2 Engineers.

3 Technicians.

4 Sales executives.

5 Accounting and finance staff.

FIGURE 1.2   Real GDP growth by region, 2013–2016 (p)

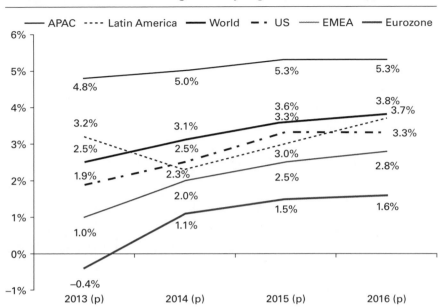

SOURCE: Courtesy of Kelly Global Talent Market Quarterly Q2 2014

6 Management/executives.

7 Sales managers.

8 IT staff.

9 Office support staff.

10 Drivers.

It is surprising that IT is so far down the list, as it is one of the skill sets that is talked about continuously as having skill shortages. Obviously this would fluctuate depending on the location in the world and the industries involved. For example, companies living in the tech bubble on the West Coast of America might disagree with the results of this survey.

One statistic that drives home the effect of these shortages is that 54 per cent of employers in this survey say that talent shortages had a medium to high impact on their ability to do business with their clients. This is when companies really take notice and look more closely at the talent within their business and thus more focus is directed at the recruitment function.

When looked at on a global basis, as in the talent heat map in Figure 1.3 from Oxford Economics, with the dark areas predicted to have recruitment problems, it would seem that the next five years will present problems for many companies, especially in the northern hemisphere and Australia.

FIGURE 1.3 Global heat map

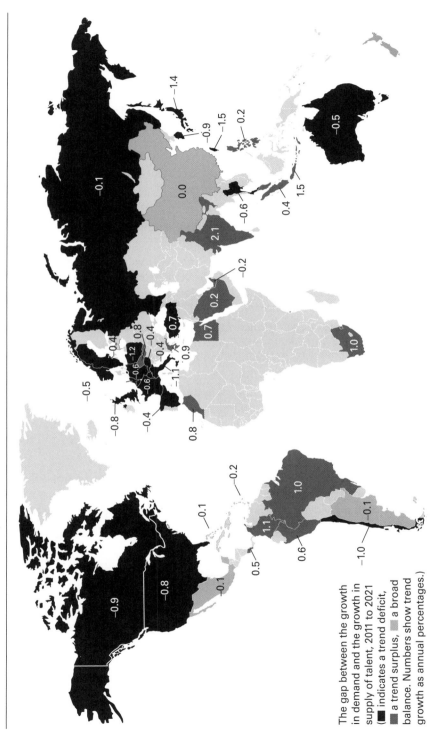

The gap between the growth in demand and the growth in supply of talent, 2011 to 2021 (■ indicates a trend deficit, ■ a broad balance. ■ a trend surplus. Numbers show trend growth as annual percentages.)

SOURCE: Courtesy of Oxford Economics, *Global Talent 2021*

As you will see further in this book, social media can be used as a tool in all aspects of the recruitment process, including helping companies to make informed business decisions via the use of talent information.

A good example of this is Telefónica Digital in South America. They were looking to expand their pre-sales and business development of digital products into potentially lucrative territories in Latin America – Columbia, Peru, Brazil, Argentina and Chile. A highly diverse region, with relatively low unemployment levels for a developing region, existing talent pools for Information and Communications Technology (ICT) and Media were in high demand.

How did they plan for this? The resourcing model to support this expansion needed to be holistic. Everyone is a recruiter! Use of existing teams to attract other people and be engaged in the process included:

- LinkedIn profiles of business and influential employees were updated.
- Social media that the existing teams used were leveraged – at the time @m2mtelefonica had 1,065 followers; Telefónica's #m2m official Twitter @tefdigital had 5,189 followers; Telefónica Digital LinkedIn page had 2,379 followers.
- More broadly, additional resources were used to target specific interest groups including LinkedIn mHealth group – a networking group for LinkedIn members interested in the opportunity for using mobile to improve health.
- Lastly, use of the Telefónica Digital Hub (TefD), which at the time was receiving over 22,000 visitors per month – an audience comprised of tech industry experts, bloggers, media and analysts, academics, stakeholders, TefD partners, TefD employees and their networks, digerati and opinion formers.

So, in this instance, the talent data derived from social media not only helped Telefónica Digital to make a business decision to expand into new territories, it also then provided the means to enable them to recruit the necessary people to action it.

The shortfall of digital talent

As the world moves from analogue to digital, nearly every function within business is being impacted by the global use of mobile and social media, and the subsequent demand for so-called 'big data' analytics. Even IT departments are struggling with the new skills required to affect these changes, due to the speed of change of technologies and development languages required by their own businesses.

While in 2015 social media has been operationally used within organiza-tions for over five years, the uptake to recruit digitally skilled workers has been unusually slow. The methods of recruiting digital talent has equally been strange, in that many companies are still using traditional recruitment methods to attract digital skills to their companies – poor career sites, job boards, advertising and recruitment agencies. The problem is that the digital audience that companies are trying hard to engage with are not there. Unsurprisingly they use the same digital tools and sites – that is, social media and mobile – to engage with each other as they do in their work.

According to the Forrester's Q1 2014 Digital Experience Delivery Online Survey, 58 per cent of companies are having difficulty attracting and recruiting digital talent.[3] The types of skills that are currently in most demand in the digital space, and therefore carry a salary premium to them, are shown in the word cloud in Figure 1.4.

FIGURE 1.4   Digital skills in most demand

Depending on where you are in the world will of course dictate the different digital skills needed due to technology infrastructures and adoption of technologies. As a recruiter you should not be ignoring these different global talent pools of digital skill. For example, companies in the West looking for developers and designers in mobile e-commerce should look to parts of Asia, where there is a mature and proven market in mobile shopping. Of course, there will be the issue of visas and physically relocating people around the world, but with video communication and collaboration becoming more common, we will see more companies adopting international recruitment strategies for specific hard-to-find and business-critical skills.

The changing demographics of multigenerational workforces

How many generations do you have working for your company? It is very possible it could be as many as four or five generations if you take into account five different age demographics:

- the seniors (born before 1945);
- baby boomers (born 1945–60);
- generation X (born 1961–80);
- generation Y (born 1981–95) aka millennials;
- generation Z (born after 1995).

Any time now the generation Y workers will become the majority population of the global workforce. Much has been written about the various traits of generation Y workers, including low boredom threshold, impatience, the desire to multitask, a 'work to live not live to work' attitude, constant questioning and high expectations in the workplace. When you consider that many generation Y have grown up in the digital age, it is not surprising that they will have different expectations of a recruitment process.

The effects of the recession triggered in 2007 have been to push forward retirement ages out of financial necessity. This has meant that both baby boomers and seniors are still in the workforce. At the other end of the demographic scale we are now starting to see generation Z workers appear for the first time at companies. So, as you can see, it is very easy to have five generations in the same workplace.

This becomes a challenge for recruitment on a number of levels, with a huge variety of skill levels, wide-range of technological awareness and personal and professional expectations to be managed. There are of course advantages to having different generations in the workforce, especially when it comes to new technologies. One of the large global banks recently changed from Blackberry mobile devices to Apple iPhones. They chose not to take the expensive support and training package that such a big change might normally require. Instead they used the generational differences in their workforce and paired their baby boomer employees with their younger generation Y and Z employees. The feedback I received from the bank was that the project was a great success, and that they are now looking at other areas where the different generations in their workforce can add value to each other.

Recruitment talent within organizations

A company's ability to find, attract and access highly skilled people is critical to its success. Yet the attention and respect given to internal recruiting of professionals and the technology they need to use can often be described as shocking. I am not exaggerating, as I base this statement on many years of consulting with organizations about their recruitment teams and technologies.

Depending on the type of company, recruitment either sits within HR as a subsection of their busy workload, or it might be lucky enough to be a stand-alone talent operation reporting directly to the board. Post-recession there has been a distinct change in recruitment strategy for many companies, as they have moved to direct recruiting models. This has been predominantly driven on cost reduction rather than quality.

In simple terms, to achieve good direct recruitment you need buy-in from the company leaders (and line managers), good processes and systems and, above all, a good recruitment team. This does not have to be complicated, and for SMEs with only one or two people doing recruitment it can be as basic as a simple low-cost online recruitment system sitting behind some well-designed career pages on their website. Add to that some content marketing automation, social media-curated content and response mechanisms set-up, and very quickly the recruitment proposition looks a lot more rounded, even on a smallish budget.

Recruitment professionals now need to wear many hats to be effective in the new recruiting landscape. It is no longer acceptable to be glorified administrators, sitting between line managers and the job boards. To add value to a company they need to offer additional skills. In my opinion they now need a mix of skills not previously associated with recruiters. They need to be:

- great communicators;
- better listeners;
- relationship builders;
- sales people;
- marketers;
- copywriters;
- socially media savvy;
- curious;
- project managers;
- resourcers;
- researchers;
- negotiators;
- bold;
- professional.

You may look at this list and think it is impossible to find recruiters with all those skills. You may even think it is completely unnecessary, but I want you to think about the truly great recruiters that you have met in your career so far. I guarantee they had all if not most of the traits listed here, and that is why you were talking to them, either as a client or candidate. Wouldn't it be great to have recruiters like that working in your team?

It doesn't matter which side of the recruitment fence you sit on, whether it is in-house corporate recruiting or in a recruitment agency – great recruiters consistently attract and hire great talent. Admittedly they may well be a little more costly than your current budget allows, but if you want the best quality you have to pay for it.

There is a snag, however, and that is the shortfall of really good recruiters globally. However, this should not stop you from striving to find the best recruiters available to you when you are building your teams. Good recruiters can be developed and trained as long as they show enough of the character traits listed above. There are many great training resources available to develop the skills of your recruiters covering all of the skills above. There is no excuse any more in having purely administrative recruiters.

Knowledge gaps

This is a real problem for companies as their senior employees reach retirement age, combined with a shortfall of services skills and knowledge to replace them. The knowledge and information that these employees hold is often irreplaceable – especially in critical industries such as engineering, oil and gas and energy. It is impossible to replace the knowledge and experience held by these valuable employees, even with highly qualified graduates.

I am sure that you can relate to this in your company, maybe on a small scale. What happens when an entire industry is struck by the same challenge? What do companies do then?

When I was in Norway recently talking with companies about their recruitment strategies, this particular subject was very high on their agenda. Norway's largest industry and biggest GDP contributor is oil and gas exploration. The problem they have is that 27.6 per cent of the 5.1 million population of Norway is aged 45 to 66 (**http://www.ssb.no/en/befolkning/ nokkeltall**). The engineering and technically skilled workers that have largely been responsible for Norway's success in this industry are now starting to retire.

Some of the companies I talked to about this had addressed this problem in a very thorough way. It is critical for them to retain as much of the skills and knowledge as possible, so they embark on a knowledge transfer programme.

Two years before retirement these technically skilled workers are tasked with sharing their knowledge with younger workers. This is a formal pro-gramme consisting of off-site classroom knowledge sharing as well as practical on-site experience. From the feedback I received, it is working well with the pending retirees proving to be excellent trainers and knowledge sharers.

Recently I was discussing this same topic with a US financial services company that hadn't realized they had a knowledge gap issue coming at them in the next three to five years. They were focusing totally on the need to recruit new talent without considering how many of their employees they had scheduled to soon retire. Have you started to consider this issue at your company and, if so, have you put a strategy in place to best retain the valuable knowledge the retirees have about your company, your clients and the industry?

Fast-changing candidate expectations

Have you noticed over the last two years the differences in attitudes and behaviours from candidates in the recruitment process? With the changing workforce demographics, ever-changing new technologies and the expansion of mobile and social media, talent attraction and recruitment have certainly become more challenging. With the exposure to information provided by sites such as LinkedIn, combined with the speed and access of social media sites and the 'always on' nature of mobile, the behaviours and subsequent expectations of jobseekers has changed for ever.

For example, recently my (generation Y) daughter found a job online that she wanted to apply for while searching on her iPhone. A link from Google took her to the job advertised on a career page. The career site was non-mobile responsive so she went to her laptop to make the application, where she discovered she couldn't apply because she was using the Safari web browser. Not fazed by this she then went to LinkedIn and found the name of a recruiter at the company. She saw he had a Twitter address and she tweeted him. He replied, telling her to download the Chrome browser, as they were having browser compatibility issues. She did and subsequently applied for the role.

To my daughter, the use of Twitter was normal. Interestingly, she 'expected' an answer from the company, whereas my response when she told me was, 'Good luck, you might be lucky if they reply!'

What would have happened if that had been your company? First, do you even use Twitter? How quickly would one of your team have responded in the same situation?

If this had been in the United States, then no doubt my daughter would have first checked with Glassdoor.com (a review site where employees anonymously provide reviews on the pros and cons of their companies and managers) before applying in order to check on what others are saying about the company – both employees and jobseekers.[4]

This also raises an important behavioural change we have seen with job-seekers that has been accelerated by social media and mobile phones – how referrals, reputation, reviews and recommendations have become powerful in everything we all do. When was the last time you made a conscious purchase before first checking out reviews online or asking your Facebook friends for an opinion – holidays (TripAdvisor), restaurants (Yelp) or any other products (Amazon)? Personally, I check reviews nowadays before I make nearly every purchase.

Garnering reviews, referrals and recommendations are now part of our everyday life. So why wouldn't you do the same before applying for a job or accepting an interview for a role? In the United States, where Glassdoor has been in use for a number of years, and has over 6 million reviews, it has become normal practice to check on an employer before applying or interviewing for jobs. Employers are also using it now to monitor employee happiness and engagement, as well as encouraging their employees to add reviews to the site. After all, what is more powerful than someone looking at your company on a site like Glassdoor, and seeing many reviews from current and past employees on what it is like to work there?

The question, then, is are you more likely to accept these reviews, or the 'what is it like to work here' videos selected for a company career site?

I know what I would consider first!

If you haven't heard of Glassdoor before, go and see what people are saying about your company.

Referrals and recommendations are great recruitment tools, and with talent sourcing becoming harder and harder they are something you need to be looking to embrace right now, if you don't already do so.

The extinction of the desktop PC – mobile and tablet

Do I really need to tell you that the world of recruitment is mobile? I mean, when was the last time you rang a candidate or applicant on a fixed landline? When you are engaging with talent, whether that be via e-mail, messaging, SMS or social media, what device do you think they are using to receive your communication? Most of the time it will, of course, be a mobile device, and as you can see in Figure 1.5 there is a real mix of activities performed by people when using them.[5] Therefore, you need to consider every possible interaction you have with candidates and applicants, and ensure they are mobile friendly. For example, if people interested in working for your company have signed up for job alerts via e-mail, you need to make sure all the links within those e-mails link to website pages that are mobile compatible, otherwise they will be a complete waste of time.

Currently one of the biggest challenges companies are having is around their career sites and the underlying recruitment technology – the applicant tracking system (ATS). Very few of the main vendors have a candidate application process that is easy to do on either a mobile or a tablet. If you are one of the companies using these vendors, you could well be losing good applicants for your jobs, as they are being put off by this poor candidate experience.

A related challenge in using mobile for recruiting is what is called 'mobile apply'. This is as the name suggests: the ability to apply for a job simply using your mobile device. This can currently be set up with 'Apply with LinkedIn' as well as linking to CVs stored in cloud storage sites such as

FIGURE 1.5 Activities performed by smartphone users at least once a month

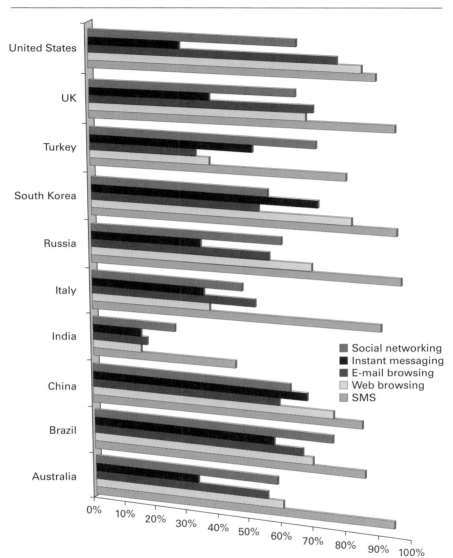

Social networking
Instant messaging
E-mail browsing
Web browsing
SMS

SOURCE: Nielsen (Feb 2013)

Dropbox and Google Drive as well as using pre-stored CVs on sites such as Indeed and Monster. In my opinion this is definitely the future, but we are still seeing limited examples that are accepted by the applicants themselves. UPS have a full mobile apply process in place (see Chapter 12), but they are one of the few that are doing it well.

Social media recruiting
– speed, transparency everywhere

There can be no denying that social media is mainstream. It has been fully integrated into business and social lives, and has been widely adopted as a default communication 'news platform' by the world's media. In fact, the latest news is often broken on Twitter before it can even reach the major news networks on TV. It is no surprise in the correlation of the ubiquity of mobile phones and tablets, and the fast growth of all the social networking sites. According to Pew Research, 74 per cent of online adults now use social networking sites.[6]

There are now thousands of social networks of all sizes across the world, large and small and covering nearly every subject you could imagine. The social networks with the largest number of users, as of June 2014, are shown in Figure 1.6.[7]

The social network that is most commonly associated with recruiting is the world's largest professional network, LinkedIn. I find it interesting that many recruiters just focus on LinkedIn and still do not consider Facebook as a social network to recruit from, even though it is three times the size of LinkedIn. As you read through this book you will find many examples of companies successfully using Facebook as part of their recruitment strategy.

While social media may well be mainstream it is still not universally used within the workplace. It is interesting that companies will use different social networks within the marketing and sales departments, and yet when it comes to recruitment, HR departments are still resisting them. This creates

FIGURE 1.6 Active users (in millions) by social network as of June 2014

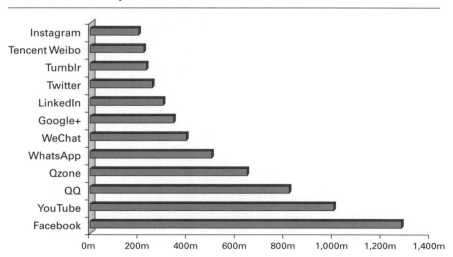

SOURCE: Most recent data in company press releases, correct as at June 2014

an interesting problem. The marketing department may be using social media to help build and develop the brand and to communicate and engage with their customers. The HR department will, of course, benefit from this brand development, hopefully attracting future employees to the business. However, it may not be embracing social media in the same way, thus causing frustration at many levels.

Just like mobile, social media is now omnipresent. You can no longer choose to ignore it, in any part your company, especially in HR and recruitment, where engagement and communication is so important.

Given the talent shortages that companies now face, social media allows you to dramatically increase the pool of people from which to recruit; the variety and sheer scale of many of the social networks really is mind-boggling. If you then factor into the equation clever searching technologies that have the ability to find all the people linked to them, companies now have access to literally millions of candidates across the world. There will be skills to learn, methods to understand and frustrations with all the unstructured data, yet social media offers companies solutions to the talent shortages they will have now and in the future.

Data-based recruiting

You have very likely heard of the phrase 'big data'. Maybe some of you might even fully understand it, but I doubt it. It is not a new subject, but it is one that is overused and hugely overhyped by (ironically) social media, itself a contributor to that vast amount of people data online.

I will not go into too much detail with regards to this subject, as I am certainly not a data scientist. However, understanding what it is with relevance to social media and recruitment is important.

Big data is defined by Wikipedia as:

> An all-encompassing term for any collection of data sets so large and complex that it becomes difficult to process using on-hand data management tools or traditional data processing applications.
>
> The challenges include capture, curation, storage, search, sharing, transfer, analysis and visualization. The trend to larger data sets is due to the additional information derivable from analysis of a single large set of related data, as compared to separate smaller sets with the same total amount of data, allowing correlations to be found to spot business trends.[8]

It is vital to explain why this is important to recruitment and social media. The world's largest recruitment site used by thousands of recruiters every single day is LinkedIn. Now with a membership of 340+ million people, it has become a huge data hub for its users to mine every day. We are currently all making recruitment business decisions based on the data we extract from LinkedIn. The site itself uses the huge amount of data about companies, industry trends, people, universities, employee movements, networks and of course insights to try to continually improve the user experience of its members. This is the reality of recruitment big data at a level we can all understand.

For example, there are over 175 million LinkedIn members located in the United States and Europe, and by mining the skills and location data in their profiles and overlaying the information on Google Maps, they were able to create two interactive maps that highlight the skills that define almost every major city in each region.[9]

Consider Facebook, Twitter and Google+ as people data hubs in their own right. You as the recruitment person will be doing your searching and analysis of these huge networks of data (unstructured people data) to find potential talent. You can use search strings and individual tools to help you to do this in order to be effective on a small scale. However, to be able to perform wide-ranging and deep searches across all the social networks at the same time, you need to be using one of the new breeds of recruitment tools – social media sourcing aggregators. Some examples of these include: Dice OpenWeb, Entelo, Gild and TalentBin (recently acquired by Monster).

If you don't have the time to construct and manage your own Boolean string direct-sourcing library, then these are tools you will need in order to tap into the social media (people) big data for recruiting purposes.

So far, we have seen extraordinary growth with social media and mobile adoption driving many of the trends outlined in this chapter. There has to come a time over the next few years where a plateau is reached, although the reality is that for the large technology vendors they are probably still going to play catch up to a certain degree.

One thing is certain – we are going to see more innovation, diversification and much more fragmentation into smaller and niche networks and communities. From a recruitment perspective this can only be good news, and sites such as StackOverflow and Github in the IT space have proved that industry-led communities populated by like-minded individuals are incredibly powerful.

Throughout this chapter you have seen that there is a real need for companies to embrace social media and mobile technologies within their recruitment. In Chapter 2 you will see some different examples of organizations across the world that have successfully embedded social media into their recruitment strategies to great effect.

Summary

Social media and mobile needs to become an integral part of your recruiting strategy in order to help you to present a strong employer brand, engage candidates and make the recruitment process more efficient, effective and measurable.

The global skills shortages for the in-demand skills such as technology, data, engineering and construction are going to worsen globally, certainly in the next few years. Companies will have to be more creative in how they identify, source and engage their prospective new employees.

Social media and mobile are now omnipresent. It is no longer an option for companies to sit back and 'observe' – they need to be integrating both social media and mobile into their recruiting strategies and company culture.

Candidate behaviours are changing fast, from the way they communicate with people to the platforms on which they engage with them. Companies need to understand this and make changes in their technologies and processes in order to ensure that they are able to converse effectively with their future candidates.

Notes

1 Jeff Schwarz, Josh Bersin and Bill Pelster (2014) Global Human Capital Trends 2014, Deloitte Consulting LLP and Bersin By Deloitte.

2 17th Annual Global CEO Survey: The talent challenge.

3 The Forrester Wave™: Digital Experience Delivery Platforms, Q3 2014.

4 Note: Glassdoor was still relatively young in the UK at the time of writing this book.

5 Forrester Research World Smartphone Adoption Forecast, 2012 to 2017 (Global) and Forrester.

6 http://www.pewinternet.org/fact-sheets/social-networking-fact-sheet/.

7 http://www.statista.com/statistics/272014/global-social-networks-ranked-by-number-of-users/.

8 http://en.wikipedia.org/wiki/Big_data.

9 http://blog.linkedin.com/2014/10/22/defining-a-city-by-its-professional-skill-set-with-data-from-linkedin/.

Recruitment using social media

When social media is discussed in the context of recruitment, whether it be social recruiting or digital recruiting, it always causes debate as to whether it can really work. There are many hardened sceptics who still believe there isn't a place for social media in recruiting. It then makes me smile when these same sceptics are busy beavering away on LinkedIn every day, not fully understanding the irony of their statements.

The reality is that companies around the world have been using social media for several years now in their recruiting, whether that be LinkedIn, Facebook, Twitter, WeChat, Instagram, Pinterest, Google+, YouTube and so on. Throughout this book, there will be detailed examples of why and how different companies across the world have used specific social media networks for different recruitment strategies. However, to show you the variety of uses of social media in recruiting, some of which I am sure will be new to you, I want to start by showing you many different examples of how social media is being used by companies such as Disney, Maersk, Sky, Le Manoir, GE, SAP, Starbucks and Spotify.

When you look at these examples you will realize why they have succeeded, whichever social network they have chosen to use. They have established – through luck, considered judgement or detailed research – where their audience actually is and what they like to read and watch. This is absolutely critical to any social media success you hope to have.

Now, think about yourself for a minute, and what you read online (including on social media sites). How quickly do you click away, or move to another page if what you are reading is not relevant to you? Look at it another way: let's say you are on your Facebook account reading all the updates in your stream. How much time do you give yourself to read an update before you scroll on to the next one? If you are anything like me, then it can be measured in seconds not minutes. In fact, the National Center for Biotechnology Information in the United States says that humans now have an attention span of just eight seconds – one second less than a goldfish.[1] How do you overcome this 'goldfish syndrome' with your social media activities, and make sure your content is read, engaged with and shared?

There is no one answer to that question, of course, as the answer is dependent on content creation resources available, the type of people you recruit, the industry you work in and the country you are recruiting in. When advising companies on their content strategies I stick to a four-point mantra that considers your content from a target audience perspective. To ensure your content is read, engaged with and shared it needs to be:

- *Relevant*: make sure you are sharing the correct type of content with the right audience and that it is relevant.

- *Interesting*: will your audience find the content interesting? Would you read it? If not then I would question whether it should be posted.

- *Appealing*: will the content appeal to the curiosity of your audience? This is something you must ask yourself every time you post an update.

- *Timely*: if your content is specific to a certain date or events happening, you need to make sure it is posted on or close to that date.

What can you use social media for within recruitment?

Due to the proliferation of different social networks and the associated tools and platforms using the social data, social media can be used across the whole recruitment lifecycle. If it is embraced in the right way, and the right tools are used to integrate it with your existing HR/recruitment systems, then your company could be using social media across all aspects of the recruitment process (see Figure 2.1) – sourcing, attraction, application, selection, on-boarding, during employment and when an employee leaves your company. You can even keep ex-employees involved with alumni communities on social media – many of these can be seen on LinkedIn.

You will notice that the same networks can be used in multiple parts of the process. Social networks can be very powerful when used on their own, but are sometimes more effective when combined together. This is particularly relevant for cross-platform sharing and messaging, as each social network has a slightly different audience and therefore a different objective from a recruiting perspective.

The same applies to us all as individuals – we all use different social networks and we all have our own set of 'rules' for each one. This is really important to understand when working across different social networks in trying to reach out to and engage prospective candidates. For example, while people are on LinkedIn it doesn't necessarily mean that they will reply simply because you send them an InMail or a request to connect. If LinkedIn is not their preferred social network, and they only use it when they are in job-searching mode, it doesn't matter how many times you try to reach out to them, they just won't answer. *You could, of course, pick up the phone and call them, which would be best practice, after all.*

FIGURE 2.1   Using social media across all aspects of the recruitment process

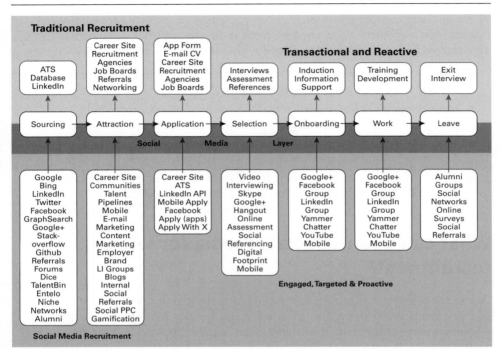

SOURCE: Sirona Consulting

They may well be on Twitter, Facebook or Google+ where it may be more successful to engage with them there. A quick search on the specific networks or via one of the social searching Chrome browser extension tools (covered in Chapter 6) will show you the other social networks they are on. From my experience, people tend to have profiles on at least three (but often many more) social networks, although (crucially) they may not be active on all of them.

Your challenge as a person wanting to use social media in your recruitment activities is to take the time to understand the social networks that your audience are using. Then you can really start to reap the benefits of social media. This will be covered in more detail in Chapter 3.

Over the next few years, we are going to see closer interactions and integrations with all the main social networks, with cross-network candidate activity mapping being the norm. I have no doubt the data is currently available, so it won't be long before we see it mapped out visually. Imagine being able to have a social network 'map' that shows all the common connections across all your different networks, like the simplified version in Figure 2.2. Tools such as Connectifier and Social360 (explored in Chapter 6) are already able to identify multiple social networks that people are in, and show them

FIGURE 2.2   A social network 'map'

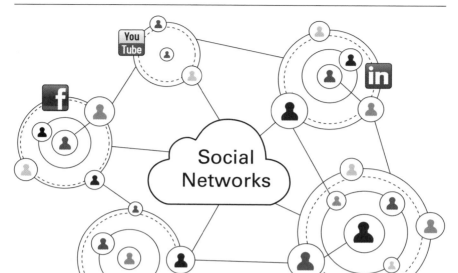

in a simple information pane in real-time on your screen. How long before we see fully integrated maps of our individual social networks?

You will see many different approaches taken across different social networks. Initially some may seem random, but in most cases they have been well thought out and focused on where their target audience is and what they like to read and watch.

For example, believe it or not a good recruitment friend of mine in Sweden uses Spotify to attract and engage potential talent.

CASE STUDY   Spotify – Playlist Power (Sweden)

For those of you who don't know, Spotify is a music-streaming service that allows you to create your own music playlists from a huge catalogue of artists, share them on social networks and then follow other people and their playlists. Spotify is a product built for the mobile and social age, and consequently uses the latest development methodologies to maintain their position in the marketplace. This presented the recruitment team with the challenge of finding hard-to-find developers, designers and other specialist people in different countries around the world, in direct competition with other well-known tech companies. While the

FIGURE 2.3   Adaptation of personalized Spotify playlist

PLAYLIST

Join The Band?

▶ PLAY   FOLLOW   •••

Created by: **André Helistrom** • 35 songs, 2 hr 28 min

SONG	ARTIST	ALBUM
+ Hi	J Dilla	Donuts
+ My name is André	Danny Reaves	Safety Dance
+ I'm a Ninja	Kamikatze	Knit And Trash
+ Head Hunter	Krokus	Head Hunter
+ Believe it or not	Péter Sárik	Better Tomorrow
+ I am searching	Al Farees Tamika Jones	Ana, Ntouma, Hia
+ 4	Aphex Twin	Richard D. James Album
+ Candidates	Splitside	This Sinking Ship
+ Who want to live for ever	Queen National Philharmonic...	Absolute Greatest
+ And maybe	Chyna Whyto	Im Rollin
+ Join the band	VETO Peter Schlattner	Metal Servants
+ Are you happy with your current job situat...	Business Success Institute	How to work Smart and make
+ I am looking	David M. Bailey	Home by Another Way
+ Programming cowboys	AL COMET from The Young Gods	White Planet
+ Maybe you are	Iron Madness SD6	Play Way
+ Enveloped in Python	Tourniquet	Crawl to China
+ Java	Augustus Pablo	Reggae Anthology: Randy's 50th
+ Front-end	Liquid Divine	Autophobia
+ So tell me	Amelia Bayntun	Blitz!
+ Who Are You?	Black Sabbath	Sabbath Bloody Sabbath (2009...
+ Hopefully	My Morning Jacket	At Dawn
+ You are the one	Kim Herold	Easy Love
+ 1337	Saving Joshua	Forever Hold Your Peace
+ Code monkey	Jonathan Coulton	JoCo Looks Back
+ I'm looking for	D W	I'm Lookin For - Single
+ Show me	John Legend	Once Again
+ You are	Jimmy Wayne	Jimmy Wayne
+ Passionate	Kind of Like Spitting	Bridges Worth Burning
+ I'll show you	Vonray	I'll Show You
+ S.P.O	Various Artists Fourty Percent	Propaganda
+ Tee	Fläskkvartetten	Pärlor från svin 2
+ IFY	GD Luxxe	Make
+ Best regards	No Use For A Name	Making Friends
+ André	Sanseverino	Le Meilleur De Sanseverino

recruiters used all the methods for attracting new talent, they needed to reach out and engage the passive audience to find many of the niche skills.

André Hellström, one of their recruiters, came up with a clever way of using their own product to reach out and engage with talent he had first identified via search across networks such as StackOverflow, Github and LinkedIn.

Competition for the skills they need at Spotify is intense within the tech community, so Hellström needed to make sure he got the attention of these talented individuals. Using Spotify he created a 'special' musical playlist for them and sent them the link, and it worked – he successfully recruited hard-to-find engineers for Spotify who responded well to the way they were initially approached. Figure 2.3 is an adaptation of the 'special' Spotify playlist as it would be presented to the recipients.

Have you figured it out yet? Read down the titles of the songs and it gives you the 'special' message. Very innovative, isn't it?

How would you feel if you received this approach? It would certainly get your attention. To take this a stage further, for very specific roles André creates bespoke playlists especially for individuals with the specific skills required. It takes him about 20–30 minutes to put these together. This really is targeted sourcing at its most innovative.[2]

Recruiting using pictures that appeal to a specific global audience

The case study below is a great example of recruiting using the world's biggest social network, Facebook. The sheer scale of Facebook – 1 Billion+ members – makes it a social network that you cannot afford to ignore any more, especially for recruiting and employer branding. Therefore, if you are one of those companies that are currently banning Facebook in the workplace, then you need to think again.

Understanding what your audience wants to see on your Facebook page sounds like an obvious thing to say, yet many companies struggle with this.

CASE STUDY   Maersk Group

The Maersk Group is the parent company of some of the largest and most reputable brands operating in two main industries: shipping and oil and gas. Being such a large global organization, recruiting the right employees can sometimes be a challenge, especially with their global need for skilled talent.

A few years ago Maersk Group embarked on a new growth strategy, which required them to recruit a further 3,000 new people. This presented the company with two challenges: first, they needed people with very specific skills and qualifications in the offshore drilling industry; second, their competitors were looking for exactly the same people as well.

After some initial pushback from the senior management team, the marketing team got the go-ahead to start using social media to help them recruit all these new employees. They questioned all their offshore drilling employees (which accounts for 90 per cent of their workforce) with regards to their social media use. They discovered that Facebook was the social media network they all used – and knowing that it was also likely that other similar people from their target audience were also members of the network, they set up a Facebook presence.

Their focus was (and still is) on quality over quantity, and growing the community organically. They were very intent on attracting and engaging with their specific target audience.

The team concentrated on three areas to ensure they attracted the right type of people to their Facebook page:

1 They used the employee value proposition (EVP) that HR had developed. All the content they posted on the page was focused around telling Maersk stories, built on the EVP. They never posted a job on the feed. They wanted to build long-term relationships with a specific audience through their storytelling not through job posting. An example of this is seen in Figure 2.4.

2 They made the project a strategic initiative. This tied them into the corporate strategy and therefore secured the buy-in from the senior management team, who immediately saw the value in what the marketing team was doing.

3 They used qualitative measures not quantitative. They looked at the level of engagement they were getting on each post as opposed to the size of the community (ie page likes).

When they started their Facebook page they cleverly reached out to their employees, asking them to like and share the page with their own networks. They knew that their employees were connected to many others in the offshore drilling industry, and by sharing their page they would be reaching exactly the demographic they wanted. They also did some very targeted Facebook advertising in the core locations around the world for the offshore drilling communities, namely Houston (United States), Aberdeen (UK) and Stavanger (Norway) to further attract a very specific audience.

FIGURE 2.4   Example Facebook post showing life on board *Marie Maersk*

Maersk Line added 8 new photos to the album Life on board Marie Maersk — with Nalaka Channa and 12 others.
June 18 · 🌐

Recently, Danish photojournalist Casper Tybjerg joined Marie Maersk to document the everyday life on board. It is not a simple task to navigate the world's largest vessels fast, efficiently and safe between ports. In order to do that, 25 people with different nationalities work together day and night. Every person is assigned for specific tasks.

Like · Comment · Share · Buffer · 👍 1,388 💬 26 ↪ 103

The results:

- Of all applicants on the career site 15–20 per cent came from Facebook and LinkedIn.
- The quality of the applicants was greatly increased (according to HR feedback). That said, the Facebook page has well in excess of 1 million likes.
- The applicants were better engaged at interview, already having prior knowledge of Maersk gained via the Facebook page stories.
- There is an engagement level per post of 10–18 per cent on Facebook (which is very high indeed).
- They used Facebook advertising to recruit two highly skilled workers in Houston. Normal levels of application were 90–199; the Maersk campaign generated 700 applications for only £200.

The footnote to this excellent example of Facebook recruiting is the data it generated. Maersk found 15 per cent of the community to be women – wives, sisters, girlfriends and daughters of offshore workers – where their workforce is only 1 per cent female. They now have a new target audience to engage for future talent.

Companies such as Maersk prove that specific targeted content works if you understand your target candidate audience. Remember: it isn't what *you* think but what your candidate audience thinks that is important. They are ultimately the decision makers.

Twitter is a powerful tool when mixed with a television programme

Have you heard the phrase 'second screen'? It refers to the use of a mobile computing device such as a smartphone or a tablet to provide an enhanced viewing experience for content on another device such as a television. Twitter is the perfect social media accompaniment to television on your second screen, as most television programmes now openly publicize a #hashtag that relates to the content of the particular programme. This then allows the audience to comment, share opinion and interact with others in real time while the television programme is on air.

CASE STUDY   AndSoMe

It is when you fully understand your target candidate audience that social media can really be an effective recruitment tool. A perfect example of this is the innovative way that AndSoMe, a social recruiting and candidate engagement agency, used Twitter to recruit cookery tutors (chefs) for the Raymond Blanc Cookery School. What made this project even more interesting was that the cookery school had been trying to source and recruit quality tutors for more than eighteen months using the main catering industry job boards, without any success.

AndSoMe knew there was a niche audience of chefs who watch celebrity chef TV programmes, especially chefs as renowned as Raymond Blanc. They also knew that they 'lived on' their mobile phones, as chefs tend to browse while on the move in between their irregular hours and shift patterns, particularly looking at short form content – pictures, short messaging and videos. So it was important that the campaign centred on mobile-compatible content.

A microsite was built with plenty of video content, including Raymond Blanc himself, and head tutor Mark Peregrine. The idea was to inform and inspire chefs of Michelin star calibre as to what being a chef tutor is all about. There was also a weekly blog about different aspects of the school – all written by head tutor Mark Peregrine. Just for good measure they also created a Cookery Tutors page on LinkedIn for career discussions – as chefs for these positions would probably be looking for career/lifestyle change.

AndSoMe used Twitter as the vehicle to target the high-calibre chefs required and drive them to the microsite where they could get more information. They used the concept of 'second screening' where TV viewers use social media – in particular #hashtags – to comment in real time on the programmes being watched (see Figure 2.5).

The series they focused on for the campaign was Raymond Blanc's TV series, *The Very Hungry Frenchman*, which ran for five weeks on BBC2 from 8 to 9 pm. They managed the social media during the campaign.

During the hour, they engaged viewers by running a live commentary on the programme content, adding in social media updates with prompts and links to the microsite. They also initiated and took part in conversations with the viewers during and after the broadcast.

The five-week campaign was a success. They generated 1,300 microsite visits, of which 28 per cent were via mobile, and they created a following of 300 chefs and head chefs on Twitter. Importantly, they selected four top chefs for an assessment, with the result that they hired the cookery school tutor they so desired.

FIGURE 2.5   Raymond Blanc Cookery School – #Chefs tweet

The footnote to this successful campaign was that the chef who successfully got the job actually direct-messaged the Twitter account at the end of the first episode of the series, wanting to know more about the role. He shared his happiness at getting the job via Twitter, as seen in Figure 2.6.

FIGURE 2.6   Raymond Blanc Cookery School – new chef Jason tweets

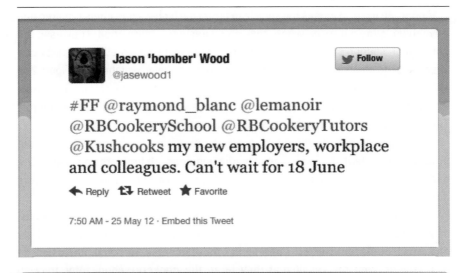

Reaching for the sky with LinkedIn Recruiter

LinkedIn is the largest professional network and is used by recruiters the world over. It has a number of products for recruitment departments to use, which are based around their three core areas – hiring, marketing and sales.

The hiring product that LinkedIn is most well known for is called Recruiter and it is one that provides full access to the LinkedIn database for the recruiters who use it. This example is a little different from the others discussed in this chapter as it takes a proactive approach to social media data, rather than a responsive approach to actions made via different social networks. With most recruiters using LinkedIn to search for potential candidates it is a very relevant example of social media recruiting.

CASE STUDY Sky

Sky is the leading home entertainment and communications company in Britain and Ireland that delivers access to more than 500 television and radio channels, broadband, and communications and mobile content to more than 11 million homes. It currently has an employee base of approximately 24,000 people and a recruitment team that is 45+ strong. Each one of the recruitment team has a LinkedIn Recruiter license, which represents significant investment in recruitment at Sky.[3]

It is often the case when companies purchase Recruiter licenses that they are underused and therefore don't represent as much value as they should. The head of talent acquisition at Sky, Lee Yeap, wanted to ensure that these recruiters employed best practice, were skilled in the latest social recruiting techniques and had all the required training needed so that they were able to identify and recruit the best talent in the marketplace.

The focus on training, communication and education of the Recruiter product was a key part of the decision to equip the team with this tool. Training targets were set and results were monitored closely to ensure the recruiters learned how to use the platform to its maximum. Recruiters were also required to sit the new LinkedIn Recruiter certification programme, therefore verifying their expertise.

This produced tangible results for Sky. They increased the number of hires via LinkedIn from 7 per cent to 19 per cent over a full year. This occurred due to the increase of over 300 per cent in the number of searches carried out for candidates. The saved search feature of this product that allows for automated updates of search results coming through the platform were increased by 750 per cent. This has resulted in a 180 per cent increase in the number of candidate profiles they have added to the talent pipeline for Sky. This has allowed the recruiters to spend less time on some of the normal transactional recruiting activities and more on identifying and qualifying potential talent for Sky.

This example from Sky is a good lesson for companies when using LinkedIn. Gauging success when using recruitment products is extremely difficult unless you set out your objectives at the beginning, and measure at every stage of the process. This is exactly what Sky did and they were therefore able to establish the levels of success they did when using this particular LinkedIn product.

Disney needed a different approach to recruit drivers for their theme parks and they did this by using videos.

CASE STUDY   The magic starts early in the Magic Kingdom

A bus driver taking you round a theme park might not appear to be a critical job role. Not so at a Disney theme park, where often the bus driver is the first person young children come into contact with. With a motto 'we create happiness' the role of bus driver therefore becomes very important, as Disney focuses on making visits to the parks a magical experience for everyone.

The recruitment of bus drivers is very important to Disney, as they focus on hiring candidates based on having required skills as well as desired behaviours. Social media has greatly helped them in this process.

Disney used the power of video (via YouTube) to reach prospective candidates and tell them the story of why a bus driver is so important to them. The videos are shared across all the Disney social media platforms – Twitter, Facebook, LinkedIn, YouTube and Instagram. Video is perfect at leveraging the visual nature of social media, showing people – in a very transparent way – what it is like to work at Disney.

In addition to the video, Disney is very open across social media in terms of their expectations of candidates and the necessary qualifications required for these driver jobs. It therefore allows candidates to fully understand the culture before they apply for a role there. Also, the social media messaging is deliberately targeted at the type of people who would best fit the Disney culture, so they are in effect allowing candidates to opt out rather than opt in to the recruitment process, based on what they see. Thus, something as simple as a 30-second video, with the subsequent social media sharing and targeted messaging, is actually a clever (and successful) strategic recruitment initiative.

If you have ever been to a Disney theme park and travelled on one of their buses, then I'm sure you will agree that their recruitment strategy via social media is really working. Their drivers really make you feel welcome from the moment you step onto the bus.

Show me, not 'tell' recruiting, is the new black

Job descriptions and job adverts haven't really changed for a long time now – isn't it about time that they did? What do they look like on a mobile phone – have you considered that? Endless scrolling or 'pinch and zooming' is not a great experience on a mobile when trying to attract people's attention for a job you want them to see, especially when you consider that 91 per cent of people now use a smartphone to open e-mail at least once a day.[4]

What about creating visual job adverts that display well on all devices, including smartphones, and can be easily shared across all the social networks, including the visual networks such as Pinterest and Instagram?

Figure 2.7 shows an example of this.

FIGURE 2.7   Example job adverts that display well across devices

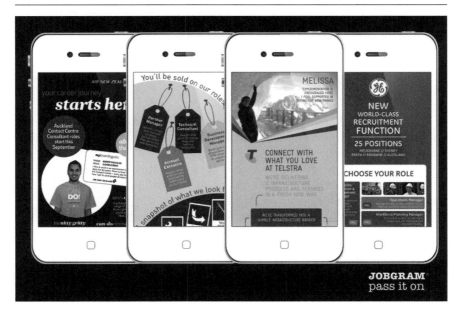

SOURCE: Jobgram – pass it on

Jobgram was the idea of recruitment visionary Paul Jacobs in New Zealand, and it has proved very successful for many big brands internationally. It offers a visual representation of the jobs highlighting key skills, requirements and, of course, the benefits of working at those companies. There are no templates as each Jobgram is customized to the particular needs of the company recruiting.

A different approach to the same idea comes from the United States, courtesy of Chris Russell, another recruiting visionary. He chose to simplify it further and create an app for companies to create their own visual candidate attraction images – Instajob. As you can see in Figure 2.8, his approach is more direct than descriptive. There is only one call to action on each Instajob image and that is a clickable link straight to their mobile-optimized career sites.

FIGURE 2.8   An app for custom-built recruiting images

SOURCE: Instajob

Both styles are embracing the trend towards mobile jobseekers, and according to Paul and Chris have been successfully responsible for multiple hires made at the relevant companies.

Recruitment agencies are also starting to use this medium as well, as demonstrated by CloudNine who recruit social media and digital talent for companies, as shown in Figure 2.9.

They have cleverly told you – with one image – exactly what the job is for. We will see many examples of these types of job adverts starting to appear, as they become more effective and deliver results for the companies that post them. We have already seen the 'explosion' of likes and shares when Infographics hit social media, and I believe the same will happen with visual job adverts.

FIGURE 2.9   Example of a visual job advert

SOURCE: CloudNine

Messaging is still social and still simple

As we saw at the beginning of the chapter, one of the essentials for social recruiting is to 'know your audience', and in different parts of the world this also refers to the type of technology your audience is using. In South Africa, for example, the internet infrastructure is not as advanced as many other countries around the world. Therefore, the primary tool for communication and accessing the internet, and of course social media, is a mobile phone. With potentially expensive data plans many people are still using feature phones as opposed to smartphones, with BlackBerry devices also still very popular due to extended battery life and lower cost data.

Last year, a recruitment agency called Only The Best, based in Cape Town, came up with a very simple but effective way of tapping into this mobile candidate base. First, they added their BBM (Blackberry Messenger) PIN on their brand contact pages to enable candidates to connect and engage directly. Then they added Twitter and encouraged people to message them by either method. Second, the branches themselves set up dedicated 'Batphones' to respond to the BBM messages and tweet accordingly.

This may seem like a simple step into social media recruiting, but it is a method that really resonated with the jobseekers in South Africa. With the addition of the BBM app to both iOS and Android smartphones, it is also a method that remains current as technology naturally changes.

The use of instant messaging and short-message-based communication in recruitment is nothing new. SMS text messaging is still one of the most effective ways to reach candidates quickly, but surprisingly is still not used by every recruiter. One of the world's biggest messaging platforms is called WhatsApp, and you may well be using it on your mobile phone to message friends and family. This platform is growing fast across Brazil, India, Mexico and Russia – unsurprisingly mobile-orientated infrastructure networks.

Have you thought about using it for recruiting purposes? Instant messaging is exactly that, instant. It is a one-to-one message that can be used to send text, images and video messages. As we look forward towards personalized recruitment experiences, you should really be thinking about how you can use apps such as BBM, WhatsApp, Facebook Messenger or one of many others, as part of your candidate communication strategies.

In China there are several social networks that are messaging and micro-message based that have hundreds of millions of registered users, the largest being Wechat, QQ, Sina Weibo and Tencent Weibo. Some big companies such as Toshiba, IBM and Google are already taking advantage of these platforms for their recruiting. They have set up branded recruitment channels on which they can broadcast jobs, invite CVs from their followers, host career Q&A sessions and distribute newsletters.

Image-focused social networks – perfect for telling a story

With the trend towards the visual presentation of jobs, companies and opportunities, as we saw earlier in this chapter, it stands to reason that sites such as Instagram (owned by Facebook) and Pinterest should be used for recruitment. They are easy to use, have a tremendous social following and are all highly integrated across all other social networks.

The best way to demonstrate this is to show screenshots of some examples. First is Starbucks on Instagram (see Figure 2.10). They keep you interested with many different types of images. They give you a flavour of what Starbucks is all about, showing the work environments, the employees working, activities they get up to, the fun they are having and much more. If it drives you to want to work for Starbucks because you like what you see, then the link to the career site is front and centre for you to click on.

Also using Instagram as a channel for recruiting is the huge technology company SAP. They use it to share their employee stories, which of course is what potential applicants want to see. In Figure 2.11 you can see the diversity of content on their Instagram account, focusing on all aspects of the employees. As with Starbucks, their career site URL is right at the front of the page, making it easy to apply for a job if you like the look of the company.

FIGURE 2.10   Visual presentation of Starbucks on Instagram

I recommend that you take a look at these sites on Instagram and see the variety of image content you can share. It seems limitless and is only restricted by the imagination of the people at the companies using them.

Moving onto Pinterest, shown here are two more of the boards I like from companies that are doing this well. The first is a great example to appreciate and learn from – the Pinterest boards from Sodexo, a real innovator when it comes to social recruiting (Figure 2.12).

What Sodexo did first in the industry was to put all their recruiters' pictures, profiles and links to their LinkedIn profiles on one board (far left, Figure 2.12). They wanted to be as open and transparent with their target audience as possible so as to make all their recruiters available where you can message them openly on Pinterest. A new feature, added on Pinterest in 2014, is the ability to exchange private messages with mutual followers. This is great for recruiters and candidates alike, allowing for ease of communication between both parties.

FIGURE 2.11   Life at SAP as visualized on Instagram

Remember I said that images bring the technical companies to life better for candidates? Well, take a look at the Pinterest page for GE, shown in Figure 2.13. Like the ship-related content on the Maersk Facebook page, GE's Pinterest page shares content that would only interest their target audience. It is all engineering related and shows a wide variety of engineering images within GE, from small to very large.

One of the big advantages of Pinterest over Instagram is the ability to have multiple boards on your page, each with a different subject/theme.

I have left until last what could be considered the strangest social network to recruit on: Snapchat. During 2014 it was one of the most popular social networks and gained new members at a very rapid pace. It didn't take long before someone found a way to use it successfully for recruiting.

FIGURE 2.12   Pinterest boards from Sodexo

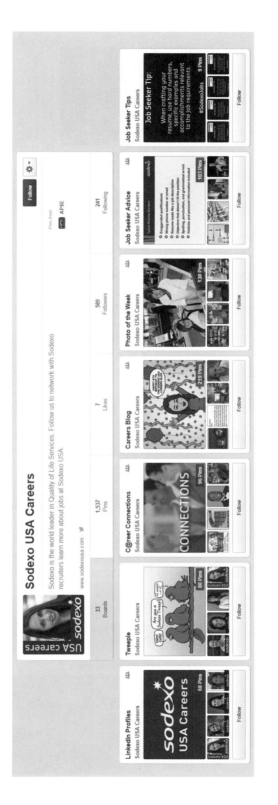

FIGURE 2.13 GE's Pinterest page

GE

Follow Board

From the Factory Floor

A look at the people who make GE Work.

124 Pins • 14,982 Followers

Related Boards

Technology

It's not sci-fi, it's the factory floor.

❤ 7

Mapping the Mind
ge.com

Sometimes a cross section is all it takes to get a new perspective on the splendor of a brilliant machine.

❤ 5 💬 3

GE.com | imagination at work
ge.com

Some workouts may be different than others, but iron is iron.

❤ 1 💬 3

GE.com | imagination at work
ge.com

"Genius is one percent inspiration and ninety-nine percent perspiration. - Thomas Edison

💬 2

Imagining What's Next
ge.com

Sometimes a cross section is all it takes to get a new perspective on the splendor of a brilliant machine.

Pinned from
ge.com

Nothing takes the heat as elegantly as our super materials.

❤ 4 💬 2

Imagining What's Next
ge.com

T K
Now it only u

T K
Could make turbine tables from the stuff

On the factory floor, there's little difference between inspecting a piece of machinery and admiring a beautiful piece of artwork.

❤ 8 ❤ 4 💬 2

Mapping the Mind
ge.com

Jolante van Hemert
Great picture!

GE
Thank you and glad you enjoy, Jolante!

Recruiting using self-deleting social messages

Snapchat is currently one of the fastest growing and favourite networks for the millennials (generation Y). Snapchat is a picture/video-messaging app on your smartphone – with a difference. Every message and picture sent (a 'snap') is automatically deleted after a set period of time, up to a maximum of 10 seconds.

If you thought that this would make it difficult to use as a recruiting tool, then you would be wrong. It does, however, have a challenge that the other social networks do not – only followers of your account on Snapchat can see your 'snaps', so you need to build up a following in order to make this network work for your recruiting.

You can create stories by adding multiple pictures and videos to a 'Snapchat Story', which lasts for 24 hours before being deleted. This is certainly more useful for companies to use. Finally, like other messaging platforms, you are able to have live instant messaging and video communications with mutual followers.

CASE STUDY Using Snapchat to recruit staff

Are you now completely confused as to how Snapchat could be used for recruiting?

A company in Ireland used Snapchat to successfully recruit staff for its new establishment in Dublin.[5] The challenge for an owner of a new pub opening in Dublin is differentiation. If you have been to Dublin, you will know what I mean when I say that there is (seemingly) a pub or restaurant every few hundred metres – all selling similar products. In July 2014 the owner needed to recruit 20 new staff and decided that 'his differentiator' would be his staff.

The problem was that the owner felt that normal recruitment methods were a waste of time. An impression is made within the first 10 seconds for bar staff, and that was what he wanted to address with social media. Figure 2.14 shows the advert that appeared on Twitter.

The applicants had 10 seconds via Snapchat to make an impression. The idea obviously appealed to people in Dublin as he received over 2,000 applications. Ultimately he hired all the staff he required for his July opening.

Obviously Snapchat is not going to be either suitable or practical for many employers, but I think it shows that there is a definite appetite from jobseekers to attempt new approaches when companies are prepared to try something different.

FIGURE 2.14   Sober Lane D4 advert that appeared on Twitter

When I saw for the first time all these examples we have looked at in this chapter, my response was 'great idea'. I hope that has been the case for you as well. Maybe some of these have already made you think about how you could be changing your recruitment approach?

In Chapters 3 and 4 I look in more detail at the specific social networks and social media tools, and how you could start using them as part of your recruitment strategy. The many different examples in this chapter to show how companies use social media in recruitment demonstrate that there are not any set rules. What is needed is the drive to reach out and engage an audience in a way that is probably different to what you have done before. Just because someone has or has not used a specific social network to recruit in your industry should not put you off trying.

Summary

Social media is very fluid and changes all the time. What works for one company one day can fail completely for another company the next. In this chapter there are many examples from companies that have been brave enough to invest time, money and resource, trying to reach new candidates across platforms that were probably alien to them when they first started. Some key points to remember from this chapter:

- If your content is boring then people are not going to read it and engage with you. If you want people to like and share your content it needs to be relevant to your target audience, interesting, appealing to get their attention and in relation to current events (timely).
- Understanding your target audience is absolutely critical to the success of your social media activities. Without this, all the time and effort you put into creating content and attempting to engage with your audience will be wasted.
- Visual media works very well on social media, and has proved itself to be more engaging. Images and videos are very powerful when sharing information about your company or jobs that you are presenting to jobseekers.

Notes

1 http://www.b2bmarketinginsider.com/content-marketing/thanks-social-media-average-attention-span-now-shorter-goldfish.

2 If you'd like to look at the example on the web, you can do so by following this link and signing into spotify: http://spoti.fi/lookingforworkmate.

3 http://talent.linkedin.com/blog/wp-content/uploads/2014/07/Case_Study_Sky_2014_06_30.pdf.

4 http://www.exacttarget.com/sites/exacttarget/files/deliverables/etmc-2014mobilebehaviorreport.pdf.

5 http://techcrunch.com/2014/06/30/irish-pub-only-accepts-job-applications-through-snapchat/.

Selecting your social networks

The question 'which social networks should we be using for our recruitment?' is always the most common question I get asked by recruitment and HR professionals at all levels across different countries.

The answer to that question is not as easy as you may think. When you start to explore social media in more detail for recruitment, and understand the sheer volume of social networks – mainstream and niche, social media dashboards, social media monitoring, social search aggregators, sourcing tools, browser extensions, mobile apps etc – you quickly realize it isn't as easy as you first thought.

To add another level of complexity, all these products will of course tell you that you must have them for your recruiting and that you cannot do without them. This is not true, of course, and while the salesperson may well sound convincing on the phone, the sheer scale of social media will always give you other options.

The reality is that you will need to use a combination of social networks and tools to make your use of social media effective for your recruitment. These will depend on your recruitment strategies, objectives, industry, sector and your business objectives. There are no exact rules or templates for types of companies, as each one is always different.

Within this chapter I look at the main social networks in more detail including LinkedIn, Facebook, Twitter, Google+, YouTube, Pinterest and Instagram. I show you how to get started on each platform and how best to set up your profiles and pages to best effect, and some guidance on how to use them from a recruitment perspective.

A common mistake that companies make when wanting to start using social media is to copy or mimic either their competitors or well-known big brands' social media activities. They do this without proper consideration of their own objectives, resources, maturity and the target audience they are looking to engage with. They also make one big assumption – that social media is actually working for those companies and delivering on their objectives.

Before we look at some of the social networks, tools and platforms, I want you to think about these three questions:

- What are your objectives for using social media in your recruitment strategy?
- What are the objectives of your business?
- Are they aligned?

To have a chance of success in integrating social media into your recruitment strategy you have to align your social media objectives with your business objectives. If you don't, it would be the same as trying to drive a car straight with the wheels fixed at 45 degrees – you will not get to where you want to be, and could end up going round in circles!

Let me explain why this is relevant to the selection of social networks, tools and platforms. Different social networks have different audiences, expectations and (crucially) wildly different data structures. For example, sourcing candidates on LinkedIn with its very structured approach to data is a lot more effective than trying to source candidates on Twitter, because it has hardly any structured data. You then also have to understand how different tools and platforms interact with these social networks in order to ensure they help you to meet your objectives.

So what could your objectives look like? For example:

- *Business objective*: reducing reliance on recruitment agencies and therefore reduce costs.
  Aligned social media objective: use social media to expand the company's brand footprint and attract more candidates to the career site.

- *Business objective*: track competitor activity to identify new potential client leads.
  Aligned social media objective: using social media tools to monitor competitor activity and identify who are following them on LinkedIn and Twitter.

- *Business objective*: drive traffic to your website landing page to promote the new recruitment campaign and attract 100 new candidates.
  Aligned social media objective: use a blog (on your website) to post regular content and share it on social media sites to drive traffic back to the website.

- *Business objective*: identify and source a wider range of developer candidates than just from those on LinkedIn to increase the calibre of the development team.
  Aligned social media objective: source developers from technology-focused networks such as StackOverflow or Github.

Hopefully you get the idea here: social media platform and tool selection first needs a little thought. The objectives you decide upon (this will be discussed further in Chapter 5) will dictate both the platforms to be used and the way that people will use them.

CASE STUDY   Vodafone

A good example of selecting your social networks based on project objectives is demonstrated by Vodafone when they created a new organization to centralize a key operational function.

Operations had been previously managed independently across 19 different countries and were to move to one central location in Luxembourg, a location not abundant with the talent that was needed. The challenge was to recruit people with specific skills and multiple languages into this one location at short notice, although they did have the advantage of preparation and research time before hiring commenced.

However, the project at this stage was confidential, and therefore needed a slightly different approach. Internally, organization design and employee consultations had not been completed and many of the target recruits were currently working for their competitors.

Social media was a great way to get started on this project and LinkedIn was the obvious choice for the professional target audience in order to allow the team to build and nurture a strong talent pool. The recruiting team profiled all the skill sets they wanted to target in their competitors. At this stage it was about connecting and engaging, not advertising and filtering.

The recruiters then identified all the groups on LinkedIn that these people were members of, they also joined them, and they themselves became active in these groups. They shared content, asked questions, joined in discussions and became very visible very quickly in all the relevant LinkedIn groups.

The hard work of the recruiters paid off, because when the green light was given to start the recruitment, the networks and relationships – and, more importantly, trust – had been built. While some of the target candidates were approached directly, most of the recruiting activities were done indirectly within the groups themselves. The recruitment project was a success, and the team met their recruiting targets ahead of plan. LinkedIn had been the single most effective 'recruitment' tool.

Which social media platforms could you use?

There are literally hundreds of social media networks, platforms and tools on the market, with many more appearing every month. It is worth highlighting that you should always do your due diligence on social network, tool or platform selection in order to test the different alternatives available. There are many websites that can help you with this task but the two I would recommend are: SocialMediaExaminer.com – a fantastic social media resource with extensive information on all things social, and RazorSocial.com – a website dedicated to bringing you all the latest new tools in social media.

Mainstream social networks

Some of the details that I am going to share with you are correct at the time of writing but will no doubt be subject to changes due to the ever-evolving nature and development of social networks.

For each of these social networks I have provided some essential tips on each of them to help you use them for your recruitment, with an example of a company that in my opinion is using that network well. More detailed social media sourcing advice will be included in Chapter 6.

LinkedIn

Your profile

The quality of your LinkedIn profile will determine the success you have on this professional social network. Some things you *must* do as a recruiter:

- Use a great profile picture – a smiling head shot that fills 75 per cent of the allotted image box. You are 11 times more likely to get your profile viewed with a picture.[1] Don't use a logo, cat, dog, car or a wedding picture (you have no doubt seen these being used on social network sites) – this is a professional social network after all.
- Make sure the headline tells people what you do in the 120 character limit (see my very clear headline in Figure 3.1).[2] If you are a recruiter then tell people that and do not be either bashful or cryptic. People looking for you to help them will likely use one of three words –

FIGURE 3.1   Andy Headworth's LinkedIn profile

recruitment, recruiter or recruiting, so ensure that one of those keywords are in the title.

- Know your keywords and synonyms for your sector and industry. These are the keywords your target audience (companies or candidates) use, not what you think they should be. Use these keywords across all your profile.

- Take the time to *fully* complete your LinkedIn profile, maxing out the character count (2,000 characters) in the summary and in your role descriptions.

User groups

Did you know that you are able join up to a maximum of 50 groups on LinkedIn? How many are you in? When you join a group you get several immediate benefits:

- All the people in the group immediately become part of your search pool, greatly increasing your search reach.
- You become visible and contactable in all the group members' searches.
- You can post content directly into the group, and engage in discussions, drawing yourself to the attention of others.

Go and find groups in your industry/sector for your targeted audience and join them immediately.

Search functions

Search correctly using the advanced search function. To obtain the most accurate searching you need to click on the 'Advanced' link at the top of the page. This will allow you to utilize the structured data within LinkedIn in the most effective way. Put your search terms in the relevant boxes (left-hand side) for the best results (shown in Figure 3.2). Put job titles in the 'Title' box, company name in the 'Company' box and only keywords in the 'Keywords' box itself. You can use basic Boolean searches (AND, OR & ' ') for more accurate searching.

Your company page

Ensure you have a current and appealing LinkedIn company page. You may not be responsible for the page yourself, but make sure that whoever is responsible for it completes the following:

- Attractive header image, not just a big logo.
- Current home page details with relevant website links, phone number etc on it.

FIGURE 3.2 Advanced people search on LinkedIn

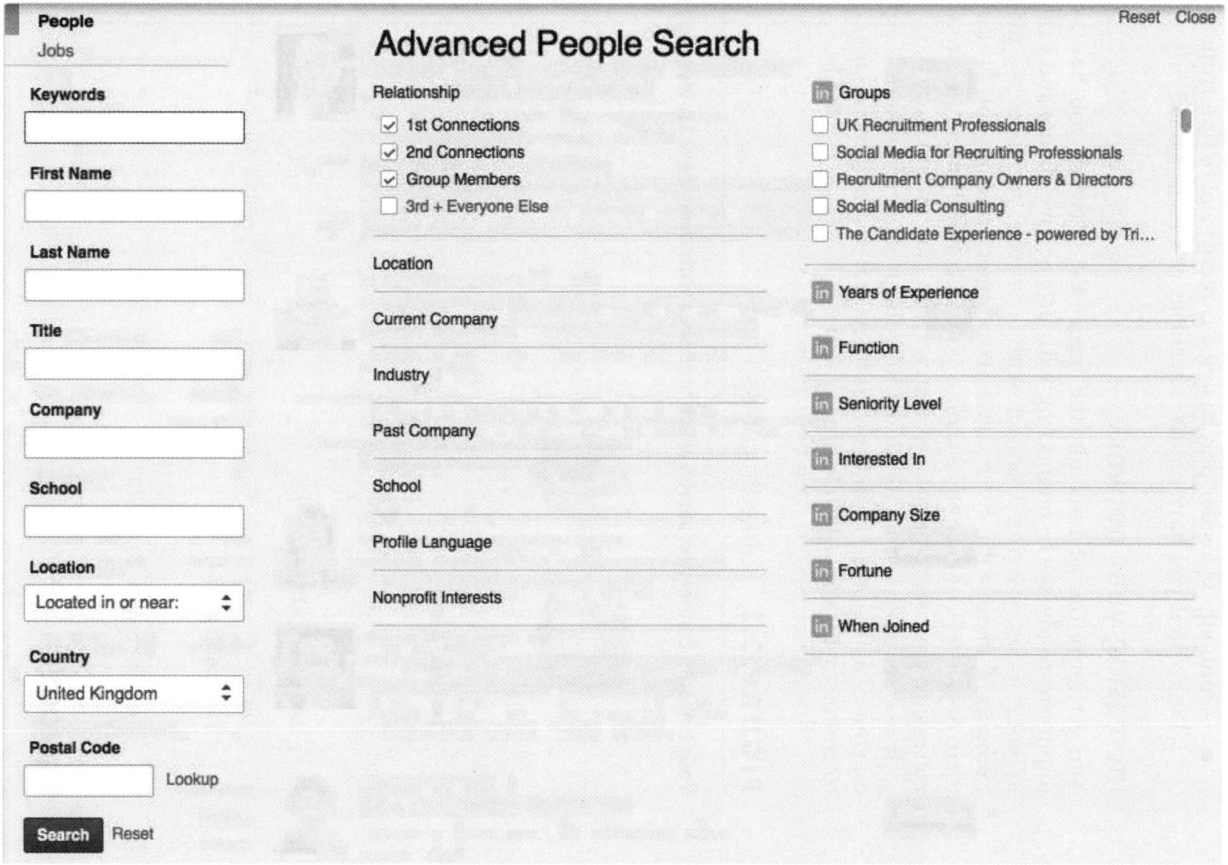

People
Jobs

Advanced People Search

Reset   Close

Keywords

First Name

Last Name

Title

Company

School

Location
Located in or near:

Country
United Kingdom

Postal Code
Lookup

Search   Reset

Relationship
☑ 1st Connections
☑ 2nd Connections
☑ Group Members
☐ 3rd + Everyone Else

Location

Current Company

Industry

Past Company

School

Profile Language

Nonprofit Interests

in Groups
☐ UK Recruitment Professionals
☐ Social Media for Recruiting Professionals
☐ Recruitment Company Owners & Directors
☐ Social Media Consulting
☐ The Candidate Experience - powered by Tri....

in Years of Experience

in Function

in Seniority Level

in Interested In

in Company Size

in Fortune

in When Joined

- Regular posting of updates about your company.
- Creating of showcase pages highlighting specialist areas, divisions, services or products.
- <Optional> Consider purchasing a careers page option from LinkedIn if you have regular vacancies you recruit for.

Increasing your network

You get more out of LinkedIn the bigger the network you have, so it is important to always be connecting with prospective clients and candidates in your industry/sector. Connect with everyone you talk to, meet and exchange e-mails with. Every time you connect to someone on LinkedIn, their first-level connections become your second-level connections, again increasing your search pool and search reach (shown in Figure 3.3).

It is essential to promote your LinkedIn profile everywhere – especially on your e-mail footer. The intention is to make it easy and encourage everyone to connect with you on LinkedIn.

FIGURE 3.3 LinkedIn connections

Your LinkedIn connection search reach improves with every new 1st level connection

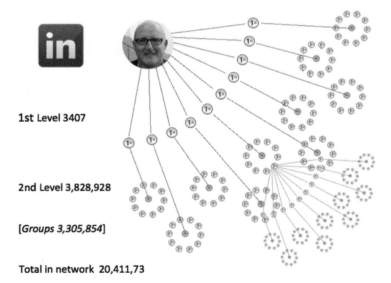

1st Level 3407

2nd Level 3,828,928

[Groups 3,305,854]

Total in network 20,411,73

Facebook

Your profile

For many people Facebook is still considered 'private' and a social network they use for just staying in contact with family and friends. Therefore the information people write about themselves in their Facebook profiles is limited.

FIGURE 3.4 Facebook cover photo for Sirona Consulting

If you want to ensure you are found via search on Facebook, ensure you have fully completed your own 'About' profile, completing all your work details including keywords and synonyms as per your LinkedIn profile. Include a similar photo to LinkedIn so that people can recognize you, but avoid making your cover photo work-related. Keep it personal to you, it is more appealing and friendly than appearing overtly corporate to people. Cover photos for companies can adopt a similar stance, such as the one for Sirona Consulting shown in Figure 3.4.[3]

Connecting with friends

Decide on your strategy for connecting with 'friends'. Are you going to friend everyone on Facebook to give you an increased network to engage with? If you are planning to primarily use it for work, then go with that approach. If, however, you still use it for friends and family engagement and communication, you might want to think again. For me, even though I use all the social channels for work, I still only friend people on Facebook if I know them and (ideally) have met them.

If you plan to friend everyone, then my advice would be to categorize everyone. Click on the 'Friends' tab on the left menu, and then add lists of people you want to segment. Then you can send specific messages and content to individual relevant lists. This way you can keep your 'real' friends and family clear of all the work updates.

Search functions

Facebook now has a fantastic search engine that allows you to search for anything and anyone across their whole platform. It is called Facebook Graph Search and it searches people's content, profiles, connections, pages you like, education updates you have done etc.

But it has its own search style, which is unlike any other search – it is called Facebook natural language search – and it takes some getting used to.

This has been a gamechanger for sourcing people from Facebook. If you haven't yet tried it, remember there are 1 billion+ people on Facebook and now you can, with some clever searching, find them. These are just a few of the searches you could do:

- Engineers who work at *<company name>*.
- Engineers who live in *<location>*.
- Engineers who are from *<location>*.
- Engineers who ever worked at *<company>* and live in *<location>*.
- English graduates who live in *<location>* and speak *<language>*.
- People who graduated from *<university name>* after *<date>*.

And you can join up all of these. Here is an example I did with a client, which found some people for them: people who graduated from University of Southampton after 2009 and like rock music and live in London, United Kingdom and speak French.

Your company page

To use Facebook effectively for recruiting you need to have a Facebook page for your company. It is a fantastic tool if used correctly for sharing content, updating people with news, allowing your employees to contribute content, candidate engagement and having some fun at the same time. My page advice:

- Create an appealing cover picture, including a phone number and maybe a short strapline about the company. Do not just put a bigger picture of your logo – you have the profile picture on the left to add your logo (if you want to).
- Add an app (it opens in a new page within your page) if you want to post jobs. Don't post them continually through the main updates. Use an app from somewhere like Work4Labs, Broadbean, Logic Melon or Idibu (if you use their job-posting services) or from your ATS (many provide them now).
- Complete your 'About' page thoroughly with all the relevant keywords, products, services and synonyms for your business.
- Tell people you have a Facebook page and add prominent links to your website, career site, blog, e-mail footers etc.
- Share image-based, video-based and text-based content regularly every day, including weekends.
- Ensure someone is monitoring the page (you can set up e-mail and smartphone notifications) so that you can respond to comments as soon as possible.

Be content specific

Share great content that is specific to your audience. On Facebook, images get the best engagement, followed by video, text and finally links. So make sure that you provide a mix of content. Use 'Page Insights' (for administrators of the page) to track the type of content that is popular with your audience – and post more of what they are engaging with the most.

Twitter

Your profile

Start with a great bio, making sure that you get the appropriate keywords into it. You only have 160 characters to tell people about yourself. I use my account for work primarily but also for some fun and banter, so I have mixed my bio up a little, but I still have three keyword sets in it – 'social media', 'recruitment strategy' and 'social recruiting':

> @AndyHeadworth
> Founder Sirona Consulting – help companies integrate social media into recruitment strategy aka social recruiting. Consultant, Author, Blogger & #LFC fan.[4]

Make sure you upload a good profile picture of yourself so that people recognize you when they get to meet you (you could use your LinkedIn one; see my profile picture in Figure 3.5). You can now also add a 'Facebook style' header picture. As you can see in Figure 3.5 I have kept mine non-work-related with a non-serious 'customized' image from *Star Wars*. Company Twitter pages should not necessarily be too corporate (aside from the logo) – and remember you can change them as often as you like.

FIGURE 3.5   Twitter account profile for Andy Headworth

User groups

The fundamentals of Twitter for recruiting are:

- *Followers*: these are the people who *follow you* and can see all the tweets you post. The more followers you have the bigger reach you have for the content you share (tweets).

- *Following*: these are the people that *you follow* and you can see all the tweets they post. Follow candidates, companies and industry-relevant (to you) influencers for the latest information and insights to reshare with your followers.

    Ideally you would like to have more followers than people you are following. For example, you can see in Figure 3.5 that I currently have 15,200 followers and I am following 6,206.

- *Direct message (DM)*: when you are following someone and they follow you back, you are then able to send and receive individual and group (up to 20 people) private messages. This is a great quick way to communicate with prospective candidates and clients.

- *Reply (@)*: this is when someone replies to a tweet. The tweet is then prefixed with the originator's Twitter name.

- *Retweet (RT)*: this is when you reshare someone else's tweet with your followers. It is an excellent way to share content and get a person's attention as they get notified when and who shares their content (as you do). If you are looking to engage with a particular person, RT'ing some of their content will make them aware of you.

- *Favourite (*)*: this is equivalent to bookmarking tweets you like on Twitter. The only difference is that the person who's content you have tagged as favourite gets a notification of what you favourited. As above, this works well for getting people's attention.

- *Hashtags (#)*: these are used to group together similar content and attract people to it. For example, #HR, #recruitment or #UXjobs Understand your industry hashtags for both finding people and posting content.

- *Twitter lists*: these are gold dust for recruiters, as they allow you to create unlimited lists of people so that you can follow their tweets in one place without missing them. You can make your lists public or private, so that only you can view them – perfect for tracking competitors or people.

Notification functions

Twitter's notifications are perfect for recruiting because they tell you about any interaction in real time via notifications (either on screen on your smartphone or e-mail alerts). So if someone replies to a tweet, RTs or favourites a tweet, adds you to a list, starts following you or sends you a DM, you will get an immediate notification. This is essential if you are managing a Twitter account, as it ensures you don't miss any questions, comments or issues as they happen.

The notifications also work the other way as well. People you want to engage with will also get notifications every time you do an action with regards to their Twitter account. This is perfect for recruiting purposes in order to develop and build new contacts.

Increasing your network

Growing your followers is critical to the success of using Twitter for recruiting. You can do this in several ways:

- Regularly (every day) post great relevant content for your target audience, adding appropriate hashtags, and you will gain organic traffic.

- Follow people in your target audience. Remember, every person you follow gets a notification that you have followed them, and will likely check out your bio to see who you are (Twitter.com shows it automatically). If your bio looks interesting to them and your tweets are relevant they will likely follow you back.

- RT and 'favourite' people's tweets several times and you will get their attention, and they will check your bio.

- Engage people in conversation by @replying to tweets. Again, people are curious and will check out your bio.

- Create Twitter lists of your industry/sector, making sure you call it something positive, eg The UK's Top/Best... After all, flattery does actually work and, again, they will check out your bio.

- Click to the #Discover tab at the top of Twitter.com and go to 'Find People'. Let Twitter check all your Twitter accounts to see who else is on Twitter. They will then let you choose who to follow.

- Download all your LinkedIn connections to a .CSV file (in 'Settings' on your LinkedIn 'Connections' page). Upload them to your Gmail or Yahoo account and then click to the #Discover tab at the top of Twitter.com and go to 'Find People' (as in the bullet point above). This will then show you which of your LinkedIn connections are on Twitter.

Posting jobs

My advice would be to have a separate Twitter account for posting jobs, making the account very clear (in the bio) that it is only for your jobs. Add any specific #hashtags and, of course, the Twitter @ handle to let people know about your other Twitter engagement account. You can then feed all your jobs through from your ATS automatically, using a variety of tools.

Keeping the two accounts separate, and cross-posting on each, works well for building a following around your brand and the great content you share, and then a specific one for people currently looking for a new job opportunity.

Google+

Your profile

Google+ is still regarded by many people as a new social network, yet from a recruiting perspective it is very useful. When starting with Google+, you need to make sure you take a little time to set up your profile:

FIGURE 3.6   Google+ profile for Andy Headworth

- Make sure you write a *full* 'About' section on your profile with all keywords, industries, sectors etc (quick tip: if you have a good, complete LinkedIn profile, start by copying and pasting it into Google+). Complete all the sections, including social networks and contact details, so that when people find you they can contact/message you easily.
- Add a great cover picture and a headshot profile picture (my advice would be to keep the same image as the other social networks for continuity for recognition and branding, as per my profile in Figure 3.6).
- Note that the profile image pulls the text from your current employer, latest education and where you live (see Figure 3.7), so make sure you have the right information in those sections.

User groups

With Google+ you connect/follow people by adding them to circles. These circles are created by you and can be called whatever you like – no one gets

FIGURE 3.7   Google+ pulls the text for your profile

FIGURE 3.8   Label your circles in Google+

to see them.[5] As a recruiter, think of these circles as your talent pools, labelling them accordingly for the skills, sectors and industries you recruit for. They could look like the circles in Figure 3.8.

Then when you have the circles, search for people and then add them to the circles by simply placing your mouse over their profile. A dropdown pop-up appears with all your circles in it, and you just click the relevant circle – they are then added to it.

Sharing content

Now you have people in your circles you can message them and share content with them. Click on the Google+ logo and it will take you back to your home screen. Then you will see a box like that shown in Figure 3.9.

You add content, comments, text or links in the main box, or by clicking one of the links underneath it. Then you can choose who you want to share the content with – individual circles (perfect for specific targeting), public (which make the content available to search engines such as Google), (all)

FIGURE 3.9   Google+ sharing box

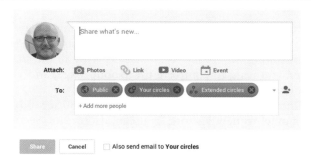

FIGURE 3.10   Search on Google+

your circles at the same time, and extended circles (these are the circles of all the people you have in your circles – and are equivalent to second-level connections on LinkedIn).

The real bonus for recruiters is the box at the bottom. If you tick that box then your content/message will go straight to their Gmail inbox for *free* (as opposed to InMails from LinkedIn).

Search functions

Searching for people on Google+ can be done effectively. Using the search bar at the top of the page you can of course search for a name to add them so-called directly. But, if you are looking for people then you can perform a simple search as shown in Figure 3.10.

The search results cover a number of areas, with people and pages highlighted. This is the basic people search.

Communities

A quicker way to find multiple people with similar types of skills is to do the same search as above but click on 'Communities' below the search bar. This will give you all the UK communities of, for example, marketing managers (if there are any, of course). As all the communities are named by different people you will need to tweak search accordingly in order to find the relevant communities. The big bonus for recruiters is that the majority of the communities are open (non-private), and Google+ allows you to view all of the members of that community. You can then go through these members and start adding them to your (talent) circles.

YouTube

Your profile

If are planning to start creating and posting recruiting videos on YouTube then you need to create your own YouTube Channel (as shown in Figure 3.11 for Sirona Consulting). It is easy to do and, as with all the social networks in this chapter, you need to complete the 'About' page, add your logo and picture for your channel art.

Create an introductory video of between 30 and 60 seconds to introduce your video channel to new visitors. You can also create 'Sections' on your page in order to make it easy for people to find relevant content.

FIGURE 3.11　YouTube channel, Sirona Consulting

Uploading your video

When uploading video content the optimal length of video to retain the viewer's interest is between 30 and 120 seconds. Obviously if you are uploading a presentation webinar it will naturally be the full length. When you have uploaded your video, you need to make sure of the following:

- The title of the video is appealing, contains keywords and will attract viewers.
- Tell people about the video, including keywords relevant to the video, and make sure you include your website URL and/or your career website URL providing links to your jobs.
- YouTube allows you to tag your video with multiple keywords, and it is essential you add every relevant one to your video to ensure your video is then found in search.
- Promote your new video link across all your social media channels, as well as embedding videos on your blog.

Increasing your network

As with all your social media channels, make sure you have a link to your YouTube channel on your website, career website, blog and other marketing collateral.

Pinterest

Your profile

Pinterest is not a social network that you would necessarily associate with recruiting, but it is perfect for sharing images, visual job ads, slideshare presentations and videos. It is currently one of the fastest growing social networks, and is very effective for improving your digital footprint and showcasing your employer brand (Figure 3.12).[6]

Make sure you add your logo and a description of what your company does, with a link to your website (you will need to verify this). You can also add your Facebook and Twitter account. The profile set-up is not so detailed as other social networks.

FIGURE 3.12   Sirona Consulting on Pinterest

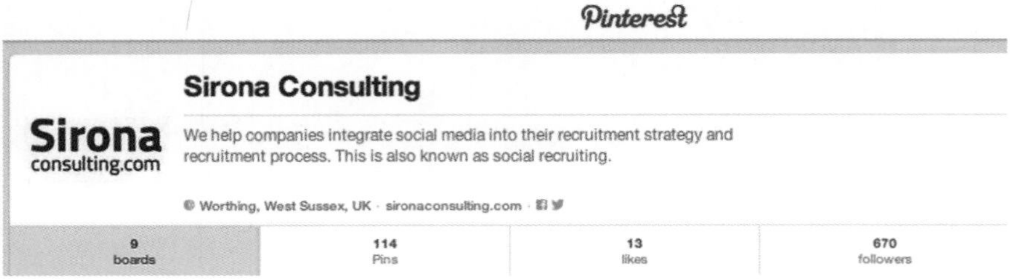

User groups

Create some boards and then start pinning items to them. Getting the Pinterest browser extensions is useful in order to make it easier to pin images from websites. Figure 3.13 shows a good set of boards from Taco Bell Careers on Pinterest.

Search functions

Search for people by name and then 'Follow' them, or search for 'Boards' with relevant content and follow them, or search for individual 'Pins' that people have posted. Once you are following people you can then send them messages via Pinterest, which is useful for engaging with any potential candidates.

Content sharing

Ensure you have the social sharing enabled for Pinterest on your blog, so that readers can share the images easily on their Pinterest. When content is shared from your site, the link back to your content retains its integrity and is therefore being shared around for people to find.

Increasing your network

You can follow people/companies on Pinterest, follow boards, like boards, like pins and reshare pins as well as sharing across other social networks.

The best advice for getting you to understand Pinterest is to actually get involved and start pinning items to your boards. This will give you a full appreciation of how easy it is. Take a look at **http://www.pinterest.com/ tacobellcareers/** and **http://www.pinterest.com/sodexouscareers/** for two superb approaches to developing your employment brand on Pinterest.

Instagram

Your profile

Use it for employer branding and show people your workplace. Encourage your employees to use their smartphones and take pictures or short videos of working at your company. Share them on Instagram.[7]

FIGURE 3.13 Taco Bell Careers on Pinterest

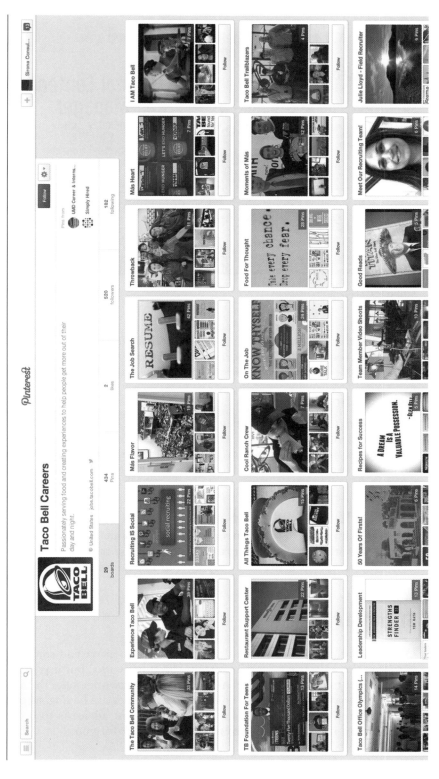

FIGURE 3.14   CloudNine Recruitment advertises on Instagram

SOURCE: CloudNine Recruitment

Complete your 150-character bio, add your website (career site) link, a profile picture (or logo if it is a corporate account) and you are good to go on Instagram. Now start sharing those pictures and videos.

User groups

Create images of your jobs similar to the ones in Chapter 2 – Instajob and JobGram – and share them via Instagram. Figure 3.14 shows some from a social media recruitment agency, CloudNine Recruitment, who find that these types of adverts work well for them on Instagram (and all other social networks).

Increasing your network

Use Instagram to drive traffic to your career site by sharing great appealing images of working at your company. Make sure you include the career site URL on your bio, as it sits at the top of your Instagram page.

Summary

Obviously this chapter could go on and on. I have given you some advice here for 'getting started' on mainstream social networks, but it is just that. As you start to get more active in certain social networks, take the time to do more research and find out how more companies are having success on the platforms you choose to use. However, the best advice is to try using them, slowly at first and get used to how they work for you.

While I have only covered the main social networks in this chapter, if you choose to use them all, they will certainly keep you more than busy, managing the content and the interactions with your audience. In Chapter 4 I look at the huge range of tools that are available to you to enhance your experience when using social media for recruiting. The main points to remember with regards to selecting the social networks and getting started with them are:

- Make sure you are choosing to do social media for the right reasons. Set your objectives for using social media and align them to the business objectives, as you will have more chance of getting buy-in from the senior management – and improve the opportunity for success.

- Not every social network is appropriate or necessary to use. Do your homework and establish which social networks your target audience are on. It is better to do two or three well rather than try to stretch your time thinly across all the networks and deliver poor content with little or no engagement.

- Make sure the profiles you create for the social networks you choose to use have all the requisite information, website links and keywords, and use good quality images and logos on the header images.

Notes

1 http://blog.linkedin.com/2014/04/22/professional-photos-on-linkedin-are-worth-a-thousand-opportunities/.

2 https://uk.linkedin.com/in/andyheadworth.

3 http://www.facebook.com/sironaconsulting.

4 https://twitter.com/andyheadworth.

5 https://plus.google.com/+AndyHeadworth/posts.

6 http://www.pinterest.com/andyheadworth/.

7 http://instagram.com/.

Social media tools

As you have probably realized by now, it is unlikely that you will only be using one social network as part of your social recruiting strategy, as different audiences use different networks. Herein lies one of the biggest problems for companies using social media – time management.

You already have a busy workload in your HR and/or recruiting team, so how are you going to find the extra time for setting up the social networks, posting content, answering questions, curating content, writing posts, sourcing candidates, building followings, monitoring your brand, etc? The answer is you can't, it takes time. You can make it much easier by using different tools to take away the need for you to be on all the social networks for many hours during each day. However, there is no magic formula (not yet, anyway) and while many of the individual tools are excellent, you need to use several of them to gain the best results.

In this chapter I take you through a whole variety of different tools, both free and paid for, that will make your social media life more manageable. I have arranged the tools into six groups (Figure 4.1): monitoring your brand, social media management, productivity, content, collaboration and

FIGURE 4.1   Social media tools

hashtags. In each of these groups I explain briefly about the range of tools that are available and some hints and tips for using them.

Let's start by breaking down the different areas in which you could be using tools to help you use social media effectively, then look at the selection of products available within each category. Though the lists included here are not exhaustive, they probably include the most widely used products.

Monitoring your brand

Monitoring what is said about your brand (and your team) is sometimes referred to as 'social listening'. It is an often-ignored part of social media, but is essential in terms of understanding your employer brand and market feedback.

You may well find that your marketing/brand/communications team is already paying for tools to monitor what is being said about the brand/company across the internet and social media. If they are, then it is worth talking to them about including some extra terms/phrases on their monitoring and reporting. If not, then you need to think about some tools of your own.

There are tools for all budget levels, but it must be noted that the more you pay, the better the results are likely to be. This is simply due to the size of the task in hand (there are huge amounts of social data to monitor every day/week/month) and the power of the systems these companies use to manage this task.

While many parts of social media are free, using a social media monitoring company can help you to assess smartly the conversations taking place about your brand. In many cases, they offer tools for you to respond and forge deeper levels of engagement. They will offer data and information that will enable you to draw insight into influence, authority, sentiment and reach, and to develop strategy by tapping into actionable intelligence.

When using these types of services there will be times when you will need to act quickly (see Chapter 10 on social media guidelines) on time-sensitive issues such as questions, complaints and, in rare cases, trolling (when someone posts offensive, divisive and controversial comments).

There are some excellent free monitoring tools that can help you to find easily any mentions of your brand, keywords, key people or even your competitors. So if budget is an issue, then these are the bare minimum that you should be starting to use.

The following is a selection of some of the social media monitoring tools that can be used.

Free social media monitoring tools

When using the free monitoring tools and setting up your e-mail alerts, you should cover these essential areas:

- your brand name including any variations (and misspellings) or abbreviations;
- slogans or commonly used brand phrases;
- website or career site URL (this will get found even if a URL shortener such as bit.ly is used on social media);
- Twitter name;
- specific keywords.

It is possible to create a search string to make this easier and quicker across a number of social media sites. Here is a simple example of one I use for myself: 'Andy Headworth' OR andyheadworth OR 'Sironaconsulting.com' OR 'Sirona Says' OR sironasays. The first two terms cover my name and Twitter name; the other terms refer to my website URL and the name I used to call my blog.

The free tools to start using are:

- *Google Alerts* (**http://www.google.com/alerts**): this allows you to tap into the vast power of the Google search engine. You specify your search phrases and keywords and it will send you an alert immediately, daily or weekly by e-mail, when Google finds that information on the web. Keep in mind that Google Alerts tracks only content indexed by Google.
- *Hootsuite/Tweetdeck* (**https://hootsuite.com; https://tweetdeck.twitter.com**): these are social media management dashboards but are superb for monitoring Twitter in real time. By creating a column using a search string (like mine above), you can find out immediately when your content is being shared or when people are talking about you on Twitter.
- *Mention* (**https://en.mention.com**): this is my favourite tool for this task as it has a superb mobile and tablet app, provides excellent results and gives real-time updates as push notifications or e-mail alerts. There is a basic free tool, but you can also expand the reach by paying a monthly fee.
- *LinkedIn Alerts*: this is an advanced search on LinkedIn. It is a free tool that passes most people by, even though it is on a platform they probably use most days. After you run a search (in the advanced search function), you can save it so that you can be notified on a weekly/monthly basis of all new profiles created on LinkedIn of people who fall within the same search criteria you have just conducted. You could use it for finding new contacts at companies, keyword monitoring or tracking competitor hiring activity.

When people use the word 'free' with regards to social media tools, there is always the perception that they are of lesser quality than 'paid for' tools. Within social media this is definitely not the case. The Campbell Arnott case study below is a superb example of an award-winning social media recruitment strategy that was achieved with no budget at all.

CASE STUDY   Social recruiting with Campbell Arnott's

When a company has their consumer products in 97 per cent of households in Australia,[1] you might think that recruiting talent for them would be easy. For the talent acquisition team at Campbell Arnott's, however, an increasingly challenging recruitment environment and competitive marketplace showed they had untapped opportunities in how they showcased their employer brand and reached out to potential candidates.

While they had tremendous consumer brand recognition, awareness of their employer brand had decreased over time. This was a challenge for the team when reaching out to prospective candidates. They recognized the need to revise their recruitment strategy, with minimal additional budget to do so.

Campbell Arnott's operate in the competitive fast-moving consumer goods (FMCG) marketplace in Australia. They initially commenced their revised strategy with two new talent acquisition (TA) resources – Kellie Tomney, TA strategy manager, and Natasha Collopy, TA associate, who both have a passion for social media and employer branding. Social recruiting was still very new in Australia a few years ago, so for guidance they initially spent time researching the best practices and methods of companies doing social recruiting in the UK and the United States.

After presenting a comprehensive business case for using social media for recruiting, the senior leadership team and the Public Affairs team agreed to proceed with the new approach. There was initially concern over the impact that social media activities in the recruitment team would have on the company's consumer brands, but this was dispelled relatively quickly.

To start with, Tomney and Collopy looked to begin building awareness of Campbell Arnott's as a great place to work and full of talented people. They started by 'tweaking' the Campbell Arnott's career site and improving the LinkedIn experience for potential candidates. The career site navigation needed improvement and this could not be completed without further cost, so they instead updated the contacts page, adding in all the recruiter details, e-mails and phone numbers. This then made it very easy for candidates to get in contact with them directly, and they shared this 'Contact us for a career chat' page on LinkedIn.

The next step was to update and improve the team's LinkedIn profiles and Campbell Arnott's company page with the authentic tone and voice of Campbell Arnott's.

They set themselves modest targets at this stage (notably they are not the standard recruitment metrics but rather focused on branding and engagement):

1 Grow the LinkedIn company page followers.

2 Respond to every message received via LinkedIn in a timely way.

3 Generate content engagement (shares and comments).

4 Improve the LinkedIn InMail rate to best practice levels and reflect an improvement in brand attractiveness to candidates.

5 Improve their position from bottom of their peer group in LinkedIn Talent Brand Index.[2]

Once they had revised their page (see Figure 4.2) and profiles, they then focused on creating and sharing content on their page and sharing it on their personal LinkedIn profiles in order to start developing interest in Campbell Arnott's as a great place to work.

As a large consumer brand, the company already had significant imagery and content that could be used – but it first had to be repurposed for recruitment. The team were very careful to do this slowly, as they needed to build trust internally in their capability in communications and recruitment marketing.

The team focused on creating images that told stories of the talented people who worked there and the culture of the company. This was content they shared on LinkedIn, in conjunction with third-party content and articles providing career advice on the FMCG sales and marketing industry. They posted, monitored, measured and amended the content accordingly. Unsurprisingly, photos proved to be the most popular content.

Tomney and Collopy then turned to candidate engagement, including InMails. They spent time crafting personal and relevant response templates, with the tone of voice again being important. These were tested and measured to find the most effective methods.

FIGURE 4.2   Campbell Arnott's careers page

Later on in the project they then turned to Facebook and Twitter. Armed with all the analytics and content from posting on their LinkedIn page, they adopted a similar approach to Facebook and Twitter. They did not post jobs immediately – they talked about the company, the people and the experiences they have had working at Campbell Arnott's.

Starting with a brand new page on Facebook, they needed to gain traction and page 'likes', so they encouraged their Asia-Pacific HR team to 'like' the page and share it with their friends. With a collaborative culture within the company, those teammates happily obliged and it kick-started the Facebook page. As with LinkedIn, it was photos that provided the most interest and engagement.

Twitter was more challenging initially, but after the team started to understand how best to use the platform, they fell into the same routine – sharing content they predicted people would like to see and trying to bring people into a conversation.

Results

It took two years of hard work to get Campbell Arnott's social recruiting activities to their level of activity and engagement as of 2014, but it has achieved some very tangible results:

- All recruitment is now via direct sourcing and social media, with significant cost savings achieved through reduced agency usage since April 2013.

- InMail response rates at best practice levels.

- The company became top of their peer group on LinkedIn's Talent Brand Index,[3] and have been cited by LinkedIn themselves as a leading case study in building employer brand awareness and engagement.

- They won the 2014 Best Recruitment Strategy Award in the Australian HR Awards.

The intangible results are equally important:

- Retention rates improved across the company for hires during 2013–14, specifically in sales and marketing roles.

- New employees have a stronger cultural fit (which helps to explain the improved retention).

- There is a better awareness of the brand in the marketplace and, as such, it has made direct recruitment an easier task.

- They have built a high level of trust and respect across the business with their social media activities.

What I really like about this whole project is that it was done with minimal budget. They used free tools where they could, free analytics on LinkedIn, Facebook and Twitter to measure their progress, and built all their success on organic growth and hard work.

Paid-for social media monitoring tools

The tools listed here are from specialist social media monitoring vendors. They are all good tools, and vary in service and style. Try them out before committing to a contract in order to ensure that they deliver the type and presentation of results that suit your needs:

- Brandwatch (**http://www.brandwatch.com**)
  It monitors what people say about your brand, products, competitors, industry or any related topics. Their tool then inspects every corner of the social web to find the data you are interested in, and constantly revisits all those sources to check for new data as it is generated.

- Radian6 (**http://www.salesforcemarketingcloud.com/products/social-media-listening/**)
  It identifies and analyses conversations about your company, products and competitors and provides real-time reporting.

- SocialBakers (**http://www.socialbakers.com**)
  They have a suite of products, but their listening product is their monitoring tool. It 'listens' to what audience and fans are saying in their discussions, and produces some great visualization of the results.

There are literally hundreds more tools available for different aspects of social media monitoring. Here is a list should you need more options: **http://www.socialmediatoday.com/content/50-top-tools-social-media-monitoring-analytics-and-management.**

Social media management – dashboards

When it comes to managing your social media with multiple social networks and maybe multiple accounts for each, you need to be using a social media management dashboard. These dashboards allow you to monitor social media data from different social networks in one easy-to-use location.

As with everything else in social media there are a number of options you can use depending on the features that you need in a dashboard. Some of the features you should consider before selecting your dashboard should be:

- Are you a single user or will you be collaborating with other members of your team? And will these members of the team require different levels of permissions due to their different roles?
- What level of reporting and analytics do you require?
- Do you want to post and schedule content across multiple social networks?
- Can you create custom searching, monitoring and tracking?
- Are you able to create and share content from the dashboard?

While your dashboard will be able to provide many more features, if the answer to all the questions above is yes, then you will certainly find your social media management much easier and more time efficient.

Below are a number of social media dashboards to consider using.

Hootsuite (https://hootsuite.com)

Hootsuite is probably the most popular social media management. It enables you to manage social media, track conversations and schedule posts on all platforms. It also provides excellent customized analytics. There is a free version as well as paid-for options for more in-depth management.

Sprout Social (https://sproutsocial.com)

Sprout Social can manage, post, monitor and analyse multiple social media accounts from one location. You can also monitor messages across Facebook, Twitter, Google+ and LinkedIn personal profiles all through one streaming inbox. It also offers the ability to visualize analytics and metrics.

Tweetdeck (https://tweetdeck.twitter.com)

Tweetdeck meets much of the criteria above, with one exception – it focuses on Twitter. It is owned by Twitter (is free) and as such allows you to manage multiple Twitter accounts very well. If you are getting started with social media and are only considering Twitter initially then Tweetdeck would be worth considering.

Social media productivity tools

There are many tools within social media that will help you in a myriad of different ways, and while they may look fantastic, you have to take a pragmatic view when using them. Unless they make you more productive or effective in your social media activities, then I would suggest giving them a miss. While there are lots of tools I have used and would happily recommend, I have listed below seven of the best, which are easy to use and will increase your social media productivity in a time friendly way.

Buffer (https://bufferapp.com)

Buffer is a popular social media tool for sharing and scheduling content to Twitter, Facebook, LinkedIn and Google+ (company page only). It provides engagement and reach analytics, and has excellent mobile and tablet apps. It is a paid-for product – for approximately US $100 per year you can have two team members, 12 social profiles and 200 messages scheduled to go out at any one time. There are also bigger business accounts.

SocialOomph (https://www.socialoomph.com)

SocialOomph allows you to automate social media tasks across a range of different social platforms including Twitter, LinkedIn and Facebook. It can be used in many ways including scheduling content, finding influencers, tracking keywords and monitoring your social media activity.

IFTTT (https://ifttt.com)

IFTT stands for 'If This Then That' and it is a service that enables users to connect together different web applications and social networks through simplified actions known as 'Recipes'. For example, when someone new follows you on Twitter they are automatically sent an invite to connect with you on LinkedIn.

SocialBro (https://www.socialbro.com)

SocialBro is a Twitter tool that manages and analyses your Twitter community, and presents the results in an interactive interface. You can see your Twitter community in neat graphs showing all your information followers, friends, locations, reciprocal follows, followers not reciprocated by you, and much more. It is a paid-for product, based on the size of your Twitter community.

Pocket (http://getpocket.com)

To share great articles with your social media audience, you are first going to have to read a lot of content in order to allow you to find the best ones to share. Pocket is a ridiculously easy bookmarking site that allows you, just on the click of a button, to save and tag content to read later. The mobile and tablet apps work really well, allowing easy offline reading and subsequent sharing of the content.

Feedly (http://feedly.com/)

I use Feedly every day and it is my go-to tool for finding content to share. It is a curating tool that aggregates feeds from blogs, news sites, RSS feeds, YouTube channels, etc, into a simple-to-use organized file structure. It integrates with many other tools such as Buffer, Pocket and e-mails, making it really easy to share the content that automatically arrives in Feedly every day. It has a superb mobile and tablet app.

Dlvr.it (https://dlvr.it)

Dlvr.it is a tool that allows you to automate posting your new blog posts on to different social networks as soon as they are published. Once configured it will automatically post to three different social networks for free, including Twitter and Facebook, thus saving you time.

Content creation tools

Some of the best content creation tools are the seemingly simple ones. A great example of this is called Storify (explained in more detail in the case study below), which takes social media content and allows you to create a story around a timeline of events.

CASE STUDY   HCL Tech and Storify

HCL Tech, India's fourth-largest software services, used Storify very effectively to create the story of their very innovative and popular Twitter campaign.

They created a competition, with the reward for the winner being US $25,000 and up to $50,000 of consultancy work for HCL following the competition.

The objective of the campaign was to encourage prospective applicants to participate in an open and transparent competition and ultimately shortlist a candidate in five categories – Ideapreneurship Evangelist, Big Data Guru, Hacker-in-chief, Digital Trotter and Womenspiration. The competition was called 'The coolest project ever' with the hashtag #CoolestInterviewEver, and it used Twitter as the primary channel, supported by Facebook, LinkedIn, YouTube and a specific microsite: **http://www.coolestinterviewever.com/**.

They chose Storify to create the timeline of all the tweets in the competition. This is how they managed the Twitter competition:

1   Interested people first had to follow @HCLTech.

2   On 10 February 2014 the campaign started with a question posed on Twitter regularly every day over a two-week period.

3   To enter the competition, people then had to answer any six consecutive questions on Twitter at any stage during the campaign. They had to use the #coolestinterviewever in all their tweets. The tweets were a mixture of numeric problems and open-ended questions, as shown in Figure 4.3.

FIGURE 4.3 HCL tweet

4 At the end of two weeks 100 people were then shortlisted based on their answers given on Twitter. They shared all the shortlists on Twitter (Figure 4.4).

FIGURE 4.4 HCL tweet 2

5 All the shortlisted people then participated in two-days' worth of Twitter questions with members of the HCL recruiting team. These questions were more specific (Figure 4.5).

FIGURE 4.5   HCL tweet 3

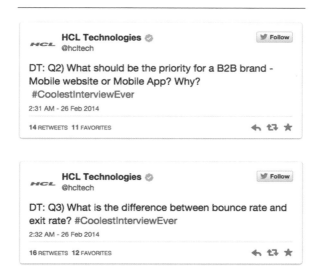

6 At the end of the two days, they selected five candidates for the final stage – this time for a face-to-face interview with a number of senior HCL business leaders from the five categories.

7 A winner was chosen.

You can view all the questions asked on Twitter via Storify (**https://storify.com/ iAmGolfy/coolest-interview-ever-a-journey-to-remember**).

I really like this approach from HCL, and the complete transparency of the campaign. The end result is that it worked and it created a huge buzz around their brand, which was obviously part of the plan.

As the above case study shows, Storify is extensive across social media, as any social network update/post/tweet could be considered as content. Listed below are a number of tools (including Storify) that are used on a wide scale and can be used to create content for your brand and your company, which can then be shared across all the other social networks. These represent your own produced content that is attributable to individuals, your brand and your company.

Wordpress (https://wordpress.com)

If you are not already aware, Wordpress is a content management platform, aka a blog. With social media 'hungry' for endless content to be shared, it makes sense to create your own content and post it to your own platform, rather than to always send people elsewhere. For me, your blog should be your content hub – it allows you to develop the human voice of your company and employer brand, improve your visibility and digital footprint online, build credibility and trust with your audience, share your case studies and examples of your products/services and allow people to engage with you via comments and opinion.

Of course, while people are on your blog page they will see other content you choose to place around the page – job adverts, newsletter subscription, new events or any publications, white papers, videos or presentations you want them to view.

There are other good blogging platforms such as Blogger (**https://www.blogger.com**), Tumblr (**https://www.tumblr.com**) and Medium (**https://medium.com**), but Wordpress has a huge share of the market and has thousands and thousands of plug-ins, apps, help sites and resources to make it the go-to blogging platform for all your content needs.

Vine (https://vine.co)

Vine has been a surprising hit with companies and users alike, and has developed into a very useful content creator. It allows people to create and edit six-second-long looping video clips. These are then published via Vine's own social network and (obviously) shared across all the other social networks. It can be as simple or as complex as you want to make it, but with a little thought it is a great tool to use within recruitment and employment branding campaigns.

Instagram (http://instagram.com)

Instagram is a mobile (app based) photo and video-sharing social network. It allows you to take photos and 15-second videos and then apply digital filters to the final picture, before sharing them on Instagram's own network as well as all the other social networks. It is one of the fastest-growing networks with a user base that is predominately under the age of 35. It has a very loyal and engaging fan base with interaction rates much higher than you see on other sites such as Facebook or Twitter.

Instagram is a superb tool for employer branding, recruitment and telling the story of your company inside out.

Canva (https://www.canva.com)

One of the most powerful parts of social media are images. They are everywhere; all over social media sites in many different sizes and shapes – especially all the header images you need to have. Canva is a relatively new company that has made social media graphics and images easy to create for any purpose. Designed primarily for marketers, it has multiple preset image sizes allowing you to easily create all the header images for the many different social networks.

Canva is not a free resource although it does have a large library of free images. It also allows you to import your images and designs so that you can manipulate them within your Canva account. If you need to create images and graphics for your social media activities, then I would definitely suggest investigating Canva.

Slideshare (http://www.slideshare.net)

Slideshare is a fantastic site with over 60 million unique visitors per month, but it is still underused by the recruitment and HR community. It is the world's largest community for sharing presentations, documents, PDFs, white papers and other professional content online. One important factor for our industry is that LinkedIn owns it and, as such, Slideshare is closely integrated with the professional network. You can easily add your professional content to your LinkedIn profile, demonstrating your knowledge and expertise even further.

Storify (https://storify.com)

Storify is something a little different, but is very effective for creating visible social media storylines. It is a tool that lets you create a story or a timeline about a subject, event, discussion or hashtag from a variety of social media sites and pull it all together into one 'story'. You can then embed it on your blog, of course, or share it across the different social networks. It works well at events where a hashtag is being used throughout, as it 'collects' all the tweets or Facebook updates with the hashtag in and displays it in a time-ordered storyline.

Vimeo (https://vimeo.com)

Vimeo is a video-sharing platform, but not in YouTube's league for scale. However it does have some real benefits if you are creating video for posting on your websites, or for private sharing with different parts of your audience.

Vimeo Pro (paid-for product) produces a 'clean' video – no adverts (that you cannot control) on your video (like YouTube does) and no annoying commercials that show before you can view the video (as with most YouTube videos). This is really important if you are looking to present a professional-looking video. It also allows you to password-protect videos so that you can share them with only the people you want, by giving them the password.

Collaboration tools

Collaboration is all about working with others to do a task and to achieve shared goals. The increasing use of cloud-based social networks, combined with the growing trend of companies allowing remote working, has created a larger need for cloud-based collaboration tools. They enable real-time multi-location collaboration and communication within companies, allowing companies to operate more efficiently.

What is interesting is that some of the functionality of these types of products is mirroring how we use social networks – short messaging capability, group messaging, mobile app capability, sharing of images and real-time expectancy, to name a few.

There are now hundreds of different collaboration tools to seemingly fit every industry and sector. A quick online search will yield many options. I have included a number of established products below that you could start using to collaborate with your team.

Yammer (https://www.yammer.com)

Yammer is actually defined as a social network for business, providing a platform to communicate and collaborate privately with colleagues. Employees sign in with a company e-mail address and can use the platform via web, desktop or mobile to chat openly or privately, and share documents.

Huddle (http://www.huddle.com)

Huddle is an enterprise-level product that enables companies to collaborate with people inside and outside of their organizations to manage projects, share files, share discussions and much more.

Basecamp (https://basecamp.com)

This is a collaborative messaging and file-sharing platform. Project management can be easily tracked with milestones and deadlines, and templates for saving time with common projects.

Google+ (https://plus.google.com/)

You may not have considered this as a collaboration tool, but the ability to combine all the cloud-based Google Docs with Communities (closed), Hangouts and Messaging makes this a fantastic *free* collaboration tool.

Wikis (http://en.wikipedia.org/wiki/Wiki)

A wiki is a series of web pages that visitors can edit live. You can generally edit a page in real time, search the wiki's content and view updates since your last visit. In a moderated wiki, wiki owners review comments before addition to the main body of a topic.

Evernote (http://evernote.com/business)

Evernote Business is a cloud-based product with a strong mobile app that allows people to seamlessly share knowledge and resources across companies. It creates a collaborative hub for your team to brainstorm, develop and launch projects with business notebooks.

Hashtag tools

Whether you like them or not (or even understand them) the hashtag – # – has become an integral part of social media, and is particularly useful for recruiting purposes.

Hashtags are the most popular way of categorizing content on social sites such as Twitter, Facebook, Google+, Instagram and Vine, allowing you to search for and find relevant content from other people or companies. It also allows you to connect and engage with other people across different social networks that have a common interest (demonstrated by a particular #hashtag in their message/update).

There are a number of tools that make using hashtags much easier; some of the more useful ones are listed below.

Tagboard (https://tagboard.com)

Tagboard is a simple yet superb tool. It is a visual search engine for hashtags, displaying results on a one-page 'board' with the latest ones at the top of the page. It searches Twitter, Facebook, Vine, Google+, Instagram and App.net all at the same time and merges the results together in date order.

Ritetag (https://ritetag.com)

Ritetag helps you to choose the best possible hashtags for your tweets. By adding the Ritetag Chrome/Firefox/Safari extension to your web browser, you will be able to select the best possible hashtags for your tweet. You will see a list of your top-performing hashtags, as well as reports for the density of usage for other various hashtags.

Hashtags.org (https://www.hashtags.org)

This is a great resource for everything hashtags. It provides industry suggestions, trends, trending hashtags and (for a fee) it provides hashtag tracking reports.

Tweetreach (http://tweetreach.com)

This is a regular favourite of mine as it tracks the reach of individual hashtags and who are the most frequent sharers of the hashtags on Twitter. It is perfect for helping you to identify specific industry influencers and potential targets for recruiting. If you are an event organizer and have a hashtag for your event then this is a must-use tool to track all the Twitter activity for your event.

Hashtagify (http://www.hashtagify.me)

This is a good visual search engine for hashtags, allowing you to search for specific keywords and find trending/popular hashtags associated with it, all in a very visual and real-time way.

You can also use tools previously mentioned in this chapter – Hootsuite, Tweetdeck and Sprout Social – to search for, track and engage with hashtags.

Summary

There are obviously many more tools in each of the sections, as well as other areas of recruitment, but these are all a great place to start. I have used all of them at some stage and can personally recommend them. As you get to understand better what your needs are, these lists will naturally slim down to the tools you end up using every day. It is also worth making sure you stay up to date with a number of the social media blogs such as RazorSocial (**http://www.razorsocial.com/**) and Social Media Examiner (**http://www.socialmediaexaminer.com/**), because every month there are always new social media tools that appear, and while not all of them are relevant, there are always good ones worth checking out.

This chapter has been all about the tools of the social media trade. In Chapter 5 we move on to using the social networks and tools within a social media strategy.

With so many tools to choose from when you get started using social media in recruitment, it can be overwhelming. Here is the small selection that would be on my essential list:

1 Hootsuite for managing all my social media streams.
2 Buffer for scheduling content.
3 Feedly for curating RSS content feeds.
4 Wordpress for creating a blog.
5 Pocket for bookmarking content I choose to read at a later date.

Notes

1 Accurate to October 2014 as published on http://campbellarnottscareers.com/icon-brands-you-know-and-love.
2 http://business.linkedin.com/talent-solutions/products/talent-brand-index.html.
3 http://business.linkedin.com/talent-solutions/products/talent-brand-index.html.

Social media recruitment strategy

After reading Chapters 3 and 4 you should now be aware of a good range of social networks that you could consider using for your recruitment, as well as many tools you could use to help you facilitate your plans.

The next stage is the biggest hurdle for many people – effectively integrating these social networks and different tools into your recruitment strategies and processes. This is called your social media recruitment strategy, and in this chapter I offer a framework that will help guide you through this process. There are also several examples of well-executed social media recruitment strategies that delivered on their objectives.

It is worth reminding you that the fundamentals of recruitment have not changed just because of social media: it is still about correctly defining what the talent need is in relation to the business objectives, identifying potential candidates, recruiting them and on boarding them.

Depending on the size of your company, legislative requirements and culture, each of these could have multiple layers of involvement (people) and complexity (process), but at its core recruitment is not a complicated process.

The phrase 'social recruiting' has been widely used by the recruitment industry as a definition for using social media in recruitment, and it can be as simple as in Figure 5.1. However, it has had the effect of positioning

FIGURE 5.1 Using social media in your recruitment

social media outside of normal recruiting activities, without any integration to recruitment or other business areas that might be affected or influenced by it. This in turn has created a barrier to adoption from many HR and recruiting departments globally. This chapter will help guide you through the steps of formulating, creating and implementing a social media recruitment strategy for your company. There are also some good examples of companies that have made social media an integral part of their ongoing recruitment.

Understanding the big picture

A common misconception (and a big failing) for many companies when considering social media for recruiting is the lack of appreciation for all the planning, preparation and ongoing work (content) that needs to be done to make social media work for them. They see the visible aspect – Twitter, Facebook, LinkedIn or Google+ etc – but don't realize what is involved to get there. Figure 5.2 can explain this.

In Figure 5.2, above the ground is a tree showing off its foliage. This is representative of all the social media pages and accounts – all looking good and ready for people to visit and engage with them. Everything *visible* (above ground) has the culture and core values running through its centre

FIGURE 5.2 The sustainable social media recruitment tree

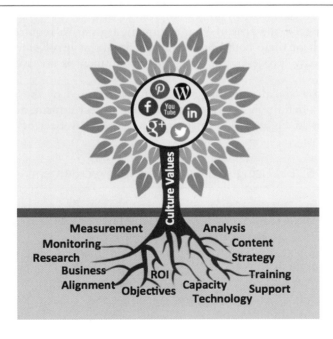

(trunk). Below ground is where all the work is really done – without the areas mentioned happening continually, the tree will, in time, just wither and collapse.

You may even have examples of this yourself at your company, where you set up some social media accounts 'because everyone else was doing it'. A few weeks later (if it took that long) – with no audience research, planning or content strategy – it came to a standstill, didn't it? Strangely, this is a positive thing because it makes you better appreciate what it takes to make it successful next time, by understanding your failures the first time around.

Technology is both a help and a hindrance

With the progression of recruiting, mobile and social media technology combined with the proliferation of 'Apply with...' tools (LinkedIn, Indeed, Monster, to name a few) being added across job boards and websites, it means that it is becoming easier to apply for jobs online. While this may sound great, it presents companies with a problem – too many applicants. Recruiters are now relying on recruitment technology to auto-filter on application, either via questions or keywords matching, in order to give them a chance of getting through the sheer volumes of applicants. These same filters are auto-rejecting applicants without a recruiter ever seeing their application details. There is no engagement, no interaction and, to be honest, not a lot of care about it either, as many unsuccessful applicants don't even get an automated e-mail rejection. The candidate experience is very poor, even if they make it through the first stage of automated filtering.

As you know, the marketplace for talent is very much candidate driven, with strong competition from many companies to hire them, and yet companies still insist on treating its potential future employees this way.

The recruitment process is now more closely aligned to sales and marketing than ever before. Automation has reduced recruitment (for many companies) to an online selection process free from human intervention. This is only going to get worse as we develop cleverer technology adding different filters, building in pre-recorded video interviews and different types of online assessment and behavioural problem solving.

With technology improving and recruitment process data (finally) becoming more accurate, you now (if you haven't already done so) need to be thinking of recruitment in the same way as a sales and marketing funnel, like the one shown in Figure 5.3.

With talent shortfalls, you need to ensure that you capture details of all the applicants from your attraction activities – job boards, advertising, referrals, social media, search engine optimization (SEO), recruitment events, search engine marketing (SEM) and via interaction on your career site. You will likely do this through your applicant tracking system (ATS) or your candidate relationship management system (CRM).[1] Through the funnel, you need to be doing two things as you convert applicants to candidates and ultimately to hiring: 1) keep selling to them (brand, company,

FIGURE 5.3   Recruitment funnel

opportunity, people, culture, role, etc) to keep their interest in a competitive talent environment; 2) engage them at every opportunity in order to build a relationship with them during every stage of the process.

This may seem a little extreme for some of you, but if you want to make sure your job offers to candidates are accepted more often than declined, it is something that your HR and recruitment teams and your line managers will have to get used to. Some companies I know have started to call this process pre-boarding.

Social media can help a company to take people through the recruitment funnel by staying engaged with candidates, sharing content with them and providing them with open channels of communication via their networks of choice.

Getting started with your social media recruiting strategy

Before I take you through the framework to build your strategy, there are five steps that you need to do to ensure the strategy is successful:

  1 *Definition.* Depending on the size of your company, define how the strategy is going to be focused. If you have different defined divisions or companies that operate within the group, do you need to deal with them individually or will the overall brand suffice? For example, a company I am working with has an overarching group brand representing the whole company. Underneath that there are five different company brands, each with their own culture and recruitment requirements. One social media strategy for the group will not work as it will be too generic and won't necessarily appeal to the five specific target audiences. So we decided to go with a number of different strategies based on target candidate audiences.

2 *Objectives.* Know the *business objectives* for each of the above (in point 1). Hopefully you already align to this with your existing recruiting strategy, but if not be clear on what they are.

3 *Existing recruitment strategy.* Be clear on what your current recruitment strategies are (if you have any in place), and how (if) they align to the business objectives in point 2 above.

4 *Capability.* Who will be involved in executing and managing your social media recruitment strategy? What will be their predicted capacity? (ie two hours per day, three days per week, full-time).

5 *Budget.* Do you have a budget for your social media recruiting? (Note: you still might be working on the business case for this if it is something completely new for your company. Chapter 11 will help you.)

When you have all the information from the five points above, you are ready to proceed.

Social media recruiting strategy framework

Figure 5.4 shows the framework that you will be creating for your strategy. Each of these steps is explained in more detail below.

Step 1: set your objectives

To have a chance of successfully integrating social media into your recruitment strategy you have to align your social media objectives with your business objectives. This is a step that is commonly missed out by companies but is the foundation of using social media successfully for recruiting.

Each different social network will require some specific objectives based on the nature of that network. The following are some examples of objectives that could be considered when using social media for recruiting:

- *Business objective*: reduce the reliance on recruitment agencies and cut the annual agency spend by 50 per cent.

  Social media objectives:

  – Use social media to expand the company's brand footprint online and attract 50 per cent more candidate applications to the jobs on the career site.

FIGURE 5.4   Social media recruiting strategy framework

STEP 1

Set Your Objectives

Agree your objectives for each platform and align them to the business objectives.

STEP 2

Define Your Audience

Ensure you understand the audience you are looking to reach and which platforms they are on.

STEP 3

Choose Your Platforms

Select the right social media platforms that will meet your objectives and find the right audience.

STEP 4

Select Your People

Choose the people in your team best suited and motivated to take responsibility for social media.

STEP 5

Provide Training

Provide your people with tools and all training required to be effective and responsive.

STEP 6

Decide Your Content Strategy

You need content to post and share, created and curated. Content Calendar is needed.

STEP 7

Measurement

Ensure you have forms of measurement in place to allow you to assess the success of your objecives.

STEP 8

Monitoring

External monitoring for your brand, people, campaigns and discussions online.

- Increase direct sourcing of candidates via social networks to 50 per cent of candidates submitted to hiring managers.
- Create and build specific skill talent networks using LinkedIn (eg connecting, engaging with and tagging potential future candidates), Twitter (eg build private Twitter lists of potential future candidates) and Google+ (eg create talent circles and populate them with potential future candidates).

- *Business objective*: track competitor activity to identify new potential client leads.

Social media objectives:

- Follow all your competitor LinkedIn pages and, once a day, check their updates on your profile home page on LinkedIn (drop-down next to updates, go to 'Companies' for the updates from all the companies you follow).
- Set up a new stream for Twitter on Hootsuite and build a search string that includes the competitor keywords, URL and hashtags that you want to monitor.
- Identify key people within your competitors who are on Facebook. Follow them (not friend-different option on their personal page). On your homepage on the left-hand side click the drop-down next to 'Friends', and click 'Create list'. Create a new list and call it something relevant to your objective. Facebook then allows you to add different people to this list, so click 'Follow' and it will show you all the people you are following, and then add them to your list. You can do the same for the company page(s) of your competitor. You can even customize the type of content you would like to see from these people or pages. Check the list once a day.

As we discussed earlier, each social network should have its own objectives and these need to be taken into consideration when building your objectives for your own strategy. It is worth taking the time to make sure you get your objectives right – as the rest of the strategy is dependent on them.

Having a clear set of objectives is something that was needed by the pharmaceutical chain Boots in order to achieve success in their Christmas social media recruiting during the summertime, as shown in the case study below.

CASE STUDY   Boots

Each year retailers in the UK recruit temporary seasonal workers to help them throughout the Christmas festive season. Boots historically recruits 8,000 Christmas customer assistants, which is a huge challenge to the business each year.

The top 300 Boots stores wanted to ensure that their new temporary customer assistants were in the business earlier than in previous years in order to maximize their level of knowledge and customer service. To do this they needed to recruit them earlier than normal. In partnership with their social recruiting and candidate engagement agency, AndSoMe, they decided that the Boots Christmas attraction campaign would start in June. By launching the campaign this early it meant that they could not use the Boots branded Christmas point of sale (POS) materials, so the campaign required a new approach.

The strategy centred on creating a buzz around this recruitment campaign, primarily on social media and online channels, meaning that potential applicants could be targeted and directed towards specific stores to answer any queries.

AndSoMe wanted to engage and inspire potential applicants with a fun, quirky campaign that would excite people to apply during the summertime for a Christmas job (Figure 5.5). They chose the campaign hashtag #ReadyforXmas. Messages were created that showed how customers and Boots colleagues 'get ready for Xmas' in the summer.

FIGURE 5.5   Boots Christmas recruitment campaign

FIGURE 5.6   Boots playlist

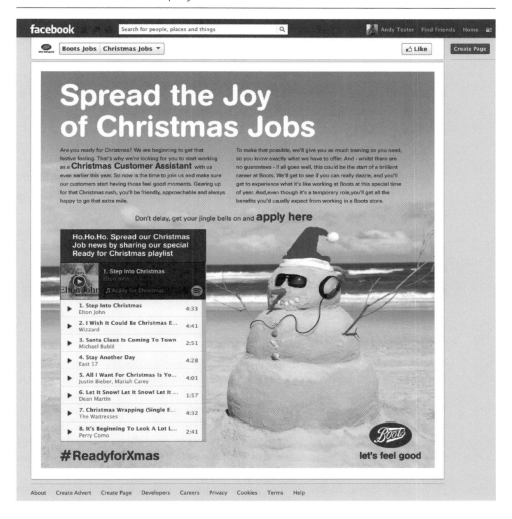

Social media was the driver of the campaign, which ran from 2 June through to 2 September, with Christmas tweets, a Spotify channel of festive songs, animated GIFs and Christmas videos involving Boots colleagues (Figure 5.6).

It was a reactive campaign, adapting in real time to the needs of 'hard to fill' areas or new requirements. Much of the content creation was produced 'live' as required – so it could be kept as topical/relevant as possible.

Social media created a huge buzz in engaging applicants and played a massive part in raising awareness of the roles at such an early time in the year with partners, such as the Job Centre channels, who supported and shared the campaign. This has allowed Boots to engage with individuals on an ongoing basis with a wider localized candidate reach.

The social media results were impressive:

- On average every week the campaign reached over 32,000 people on Twitter alone – averaging 50+ retweets per week.

- The average post on Facebook received between 25 and 55 likes and reached 65,000+ people. They only posted one update per week.

- It also averaged over 120 views on each of the animated Christmas GIFs on Twitpic.

This campaign was a first for Boots, in both timing and in the choice of media channels used – and has proved a massively successful strategy that will be repeated if the same recruitment approach is needed again.

The campaign received 303,806 applications and filled all 8,000 vacancies at a significantly lower cost per hire than previous years (done in the normal 'Xmas recruitment' season of September onwards.)

Step 2: define your audience

This is a critical part of making your social media success in recruitment. If you have not defined your target audience that you want to reach out to, target and engage with, you will be wasting all your social media activities. When you are recruiting, you should have a good profile of the types of people you would like to attract to your company (active candidates), and the individuals you would like to target (passive candidates). Social media is based primarily on unstructured and user-generated data – a rare exception to this is LinkedIn, with their structured data format.

You are going to try to find and identify people on social media from information they post in their bio, updates that they share and groups/ communities that they belong to. Due to the unstructured nature of social networks, you cannot rely on people to use job titles, company names or recognized industry keywords to describe themselves. Due to the limited characters allowed on social network bios, it is more common for people to use different words and synonyms to describe what they are and what they do. The better you are at profiling your target audience, the more success you will have in recruiting them in the future.

Here are some tips to help you build your detailed profile of the audience you want to target:

- List all the common job titles you hire/recruit for into a spreadsheet. Then add the synonyms of these job titles. Remember: it is user-generated content, so it isn't just what you call the jobs, it is what people refer to them as. This is *really* important as many companies use weird and wonderful job titles that are unique to them and are not commonly used by other companies or jobseekers. A great example of this is from the recruitment industry: a job title widely used by companies to describe their recruiters is Talent Acquisition Manager. Yet, if you were looking for a recruiter would you search for that title or would your search include recruitment, recruiter or recruitment consultant? When you have put this on a spreadsheet make sure you save it in a central drive or file for your team.

● List all the primary keywords associated with these same job titles and, as above, add them and their synonyms to your spreadsheet. These are the keywords that you would expect to see in profiles, bios, online resumes, etc.

● A good tool to use to help with alternative keywords and synonyms is the Google Keyword Planner. You will need a Google AdWords account for access, but with it you can perform many of the same research tasks that the Keyword Tool provides for revealing related phrases, popularity counts and competitive search rankings.

Here is an example of what I mean for a sales job (there are many common phrases that could define the same job, depending on the size of the company): sales executive, sales representative, sales account manager, account manager, business development manager, sales manager, sales exec, sales rep, sales and marketing executive, head of sales, sales director.

Remember: at this stage you are not sourcing yet, you are at the identification stage of how your target audience refers to itself.

Step 3: choose your platforms

After finishing steps 1 and 2 this third step completes your research phase. Now you know your objectives, the best-suited social media sites for achieving certain objectives and all your defined audience profile information, it is time to work out the best social media networks to get started with.

My advice for this step would be to also involve your existing employees (or candidates if you are a recruitment agency) in helping you figure this out. They will represent the types of people you want to hire for your company, so if you can find out which social networks, groups and communities they are users of, then it will help to give you a great indicator of social networks to start with for your recruiting activities.

So ask them the questions via e-mail or an anonymous survey tool (such as Survey Monkey). Which social networks are you a member of? Which of them are you most active on? Where do you have most conversations with your (skills) peer group?

The secret is not to prompt them with choices or drop-down lists, let them tell you, and you will get some interesting results. Just make sure you get as many employees to answer – they are the best source of this information.

While you are waiting to get the answers back from them, here are a few other methods you could use to identify the correct networks:

- Build some basic search strings and start applying them to the main networks such as LinkedIn, Facebook, Twitter, Google+, YouTube, Pinterest, Quora and Slideshare. If you have IT/technical roles then it is likely that you also need to look at Github and StackOverflow. This will give you a good feel as to where you should start focusing your efforts.

- Use LinkedIn to help identify suitable groups of your target audience. On LinkedIn the average number of groups per member is seven. Check out the profiles of a number of potentially good examples of your target audience, scroll to the bottom of their profiles and see what groups they are in. Obviously you then have a great starting point to find similar people to engage with.

- If you have the knowledge, then you might find it easier using a Boolean search string to look at the sites in more detail (more on this in Chapter 6).

Remember, you don't have to use all the different social media networks just because you can. Starting with a small number at the beginning will be more beneficial.

Step 4: select your people

Over the last couple of years, as companies have made the move into social media, I have seen an error trend that it is important not to replicate. The trend was to appoint a new graduate or intern to be responsible for the company's social media activities. This was based on the belief that all graduates 'know' social media, making them 'perfect' candidates for the roles. In my experience this is wrong on a number of counts and can actually damage your social media efforts. Here's why:

- Contrary to expectations, most graduates only have a limited knowledge of social media, eg Facebook and/or Twitter. Their experience is understandably limited to responding to their friends and their own social groups, and sharing content between them.
    While this may sound great initially, as they may well seem to have more experience than anyone in your team, the problem is the shallowness of the conversation. They often have never had to reach out to new people for the first time and engage with them in a meaningful way. Then when this needs further 'conversation' they don't have the depth of work experience to be able to do this.

- They have little or no experience of using one of the primary social networks that most companies use for recruiting – LinkedIn. For me, this is important because it is an important part of the social recruitment mix for finding people, 'cross-referencing' their profiles, contacting them and credibility purposes (depth of profile and relevant experience).

- It is likely they will have no recruiting experience/knowledge with which to identify suitable opportunities for timely discussion.
- They have no knowledge of your company, brand and culture. Would you risk having someone like this as the 'social face' of your social media activities?
- What content are they going to post? Are you expecting them to write content about your company (see above point), your employees, success stories, news, etc? Are you expecting them to create, manage and facilitate a full content calendar with cross-company contributions? Is that realistic?

My advice to companies when trying to select people to take up these types of roles is to identify employees within your team who are active on social media. They will have an affinity with specific social networks, enjoy using them and will be more likely to want to add this to their day job. However, I recently had experience of two companies that had told several employees they were going to be responsible for the company's social media activities, based on their social media use outside work. After a few weeks it wasn't working, and when I asked them why that was the case, it turned out they used it as an escape from work because they were unhappy in their jobs. Then having to use it for work just made it even worse.

There are a number of roles you will need to fulfil with social media, and while these may well prove to be the same person initially, they will need to be developed in time. You will need content providers, moderators and community managers who will facilitate the discussions and engagement. It would be advisable to have at least two people involved in your social media efforts, as there will be weekend and evening monitoring/responses required – as social media is continually on.

Also, it is important not to forget all your other employees. Get them involved by actively encouraging them to share, like and comment on posts, updates and content. This not only demonstrates an engaged workforce but it also provides a wider reach (through their networks) for your brand.

When you have selected the people, it is essential that you give them the tools to do their job, both inside and outside working hours. That means a laptop, a smartphone or tablet that has the relevant apps of the networks and platforms you use.

Step 5: provide training

Training comes in two parts. The first is the training that can be provided by every social media network and tool/platform. It is essential to make sure that all the people selected understand how to use the platforms effectively. Sometimes this will be on-demand self-learning video training. The second part of the training should be provided by an independent trainer with specific experience of using social media for the tasks you plan to use it for, ie recruiting, branding, content marketing, candidate sourcing, etc.

The reason I say this is that these trainers will have specific experience of how to use the different social networks for those tasks, which has built up over time. A day's training can provide a good shortcut to learning some useful tips, tricks and methods to improve your social media activities.

Step 6: decide your content strategy

This is dependent on all the above factors – objectives, your audience, which social networks you use and the people you have producing the content for you. Even if you have a wealth of your own content to share every day, you will also need to consider curating and sharing relevant external content with your audiences. It may seem strange recommending that you share content from other companies, but as long as you add comment or frame the discussion as to why people should read the article/watch the video, it can actually enhance your reputation in your industry/sector. For example, I know (*because people tell me*) I get many new followers on my Twitter account (@andyheadworth) due to the variety of good content I share. I usually share and retweet six or seven articles every day, and only one of them will be an article I have written (on my blog). I don't just randomly select content, I carefully read and select articles and posts I think my audience will find interesting and relevant.

There are many different types of content that you can share across social media, for example: stories, pictures, video, micro-video (Vine and Instagram), podcasts, presentations, case studies, reports, white papers, interviews, info-graphics, studies, latest news, blogs, industry news *and many more*.

When you have created one piece of content, you should then be looking at repurposing it in different ways to ensure you are maximizing the time and effort spent creating it originally. A good blog post could also become a slide deck presentation, an audio podcast, a video and an infographic.

You then realize that creating a content strategy becomes vitally important. With a content strategy comes the need for producing a content calendar, usually 30 days in advance, which allows you to schedule and manage content being posted across all your social platforms. Whatever your content strategy you will need to ensure that the reader experience across different social media networks maintains a consistent brand identity – tone of voice, style, colours, header images, logos, etc.

Step 7: measurement

Measurement brings meaning and context to your social media recruiting efforts. Without it you will have absolutely no idea as to the success (or failure) of all your activities. Obviously your objectives will dictate your measurement, and these should (ideally) be considered in tandem when creating your strategy. You need to make sure that you have forms of measurement in place from the beginning, depending on the objectives. One absolute basic minimum is to have a website analytics tool in place that allows you to analyse your social media and mobile traffic to your career website. Other areas of measurement could be:

- Tracking the growth of your social media networks via the increases in people following you, fans, likes, subscribers, etc.
- Measuring levels of interaction by the number (and quality) of blog post comments, mentions and replies on Twitter, comments and shares on Facebook, etc.
- Defining recruitment job advertising success via social media can be tracked using tracking codes or URLs, which can be identified in the analytics of a career site in order to establish whether they are driving applications.

Different levels of management within a company will require different levels of measurement. Ultimately there is one metric that everyone talks about when social media is concerned, and that is the return on investment (ROI).

For recruitment purposes, automated (candidate) source tracking is the most effective way to understand where candidates and hires come from. In many companies this is still performed by candidates ticking a 'where did you hear about this job?' drop-down box themselves during the application process, making it a guide as opposed to a hard metric. This is becoming easier to do as recruitment software vendors (ATS and CRM) are finally beginning to understand social media source tracking.

Step 8: monitoring

Social media monitoring is also referred to as social media listening, and is a really important part of your strategy. In simple terms, it is the process of identifying and assessing what is being said about you, your company, product, service or brand across the social media channels.

At some stage it is guaranteed that people will talk about something to do with your company – good or bad. It might be something as simple as resharing some of your own created content, or it might well be applicants or candidates voicing their displeasure during their recruitment process. Whatever it is, it is crucial that you use some form of social media monitoring tool to capture this 'social media intelligence'. There are many tools that can help you to do this (covered in Chapter 4), depending on your budget.

Social media monitoring can also be used as an excellent insight and intelligence tool, searching for specific terms, people, keywords, phrases and industry terms across many different forms of social media.

For example, I use a tool called Mention to monitor when and where my blog posts get shared (that I don't see on Twitter), as I have had some plagiarism issues of my posts in the past. For example, via Mention, I discovered that an Asian job board was blatantly copying my blog posts without permission and without any attribution. They have since removed them.

If you are a company that is looking to get started with social media for recruiting for the first time, then this may all look a little imposing for you. My advice is always to start small and build up from there. So if you know that Twitter is a platform where your audience is, then take the time to actively focus on that one platform to start with. It is better for your brand and candidate engagement to have one or two strong performing social networks than five or six that you use once or twice a month.

If you have done your research into your audience, then you might choose only to focus on one platform, which is what the City of Edmonton did for their recruitment, as shown in the case study below.

CASE STUDY   City of Edmonton, Alberta, Canada

When your organization is already an employer of choice, making changes to your recruitment strategy is a risk, however calculated it is. But this is exactly what the City of Edmonton, Alberta, Canada did to (ultimately) great effect.

The recruiting team, led by Shahid Wazed, became more aware of negative feedback from job applicants about recruitment experiences they were having applying for jobs in general in Canada. Applicants were sending CVs via ATSs, receiving no feedback and having no contact with recruiters, other than automated e-mails. The team recognized this as an opportunity to further confirm City of Edmonton as an employer of choice and at the same time provide them with a new access to potential candidates, which was important with the tightening of the job market and candidate availability in western Canada.

Wazed had previously carried out a research project on how different companies had been using Facebook for recruiting, and proposed they use Facebook at the City of Edmonton for recruiting, employer branding and candidate engagement. They set up and launched a 'City of Edmonton Jobs' Facebook page (as seen in Figure 5.7). The recruitment team hosted live job-search webinars to engage and inform people with regards to everything they needed to know when seeking employment with the City of Edmonton.

They also hosted live 'Ask a Recruiter' sessions every week at a set time on their Facebook page, giving direct access to the recruiters, as well as providing transparency into the recruiting process. This approach of providing jobseekers with regular live question-and-answer sessions was the first in its kind across Canada and proved very popular. They took this a stage further through Facebook by giving jobseekers an opportunity to win a one-on-one coaching session with a City of Edmonton recruiter every month. Through these monthly coaching sessions, the winners received personalized advice from the recruiters.

FIGURE 5.7   City of Edmonton recruitment on Facebook

The final part of their innovative approach, and again a first for Canada, was to host a City of Edmonton Career Fair on Facebook, by giving real-time access to hiring managers on Facebook during the event, for jobseekers across Canada to explore work opportunities in Edmonton.

To extend the reach of their new Facebook page, they encouraged existing Edmonton employees to like and share the page, asked jobseekers to further share it with their friends as well as creating targeted Facebook advertising campaigns to drive jobseekers to the page. They used the Work4Labs Facebook application within the Facebook page, allowing them to have full job posting, job search and apply functionality within their page. By adding videos from employees it makes it a welcoming and informing place to find information and jobs in the City of Edmonton (Figure 5.8).

Results

Within the first year, the recruitment team made 28 hires directly from Facebook, and Facebook became the second-highest source of hire. They have built a large active community on Facebook with over 67,000 page likes. They discovered that monthly traffic levels to the City of Edmonton's career site was elevated to 42 per cent via mobile devices, highlighting the increasing use of mobile devices by today's jobseekers.

There were some intangible benefits as well. The City of Edmonton became seen as a helpful employer that cares about people, which has improved their employment brand. The word-of-mouth resonance has been strong, with jobseekers very happy to share content and refer people to Edmonton.

FIGURE 5.8 Facebook page for City of Edmonton Jobs

Executive Director/Superintendent, Human Resource Division

City of Edmonton was also awarded the Thomas H. Muehlenbeck Award for its 'City of Edmonton Jobs' Facebook page, for Excellence in local government by the Alliance for Innovation, competing with over 100 municipalities from across North America.[2]

Summary

As you have seen in this chapter, there is work to be done when you wish to consider using social media for recruiting. It is not as simple as just using a social network and posting some updates or tweets. The two examples I used, Boots and City of Edmonton, as well as Campbell Arnott's in Chapter 4, were all successful because each of the companies had made sure they had done their initial research. They knew where their target audiences were and what would engage them – and they executed their strategies accordingly. They all achieved their objectives. In Chapter 6 this strategy is turned around, with the objectives becoming specific people, as we look at how to source candidates on the social networks.

Make sure that you keep focused on these aspects of your social media strategy:

- Remember that every touch point a candidate has with you during a recruiting process is an opportunity to build a positive impression about your company.

- Be clear about your objectives for using social media for your recruiting, and wherever possible align them to the business objectives.

- Do not use more social networks than you need to. If your audience is primarily on Facebook, focus on that first, just as the City of Edmonton did to good effect. Prioritizing your time and resources will help you to succeed.

Notes

1 Note the name change from 'customer' to 'candidate' (people usually know CRMs as the former).

2 http://transformgov.org/en/about/innovation_awards.

Candidate sourcing with social media

There are many people in the recruitment industry who associate social media recruiting directly with sourcing candidates via social media. It is of course one of the ways you can use it, and it can be very effective for identifying and sourcing prospective candidates.

I have been working around the talent attraction and sourcing space in recruitment for many years and have got to know some really great sourcing professionals around the world. While I am not a bad talent sourcer myself, I thought I would ask a number of the best sourcers in the world to share some of their wisdom in this book, and they kindly obliged. In this chapter we have some superb sourcing knowledge from the United States, the UK, the Netherlands, Ireland and India, looking at sourcing candidates via LinkedIn, Facebook, Twitter, Google+, video, images and internationally, X-ray searching and using web browser extensions. Before encountering the combined wisdom of all these 'super sourcers' let's break down what we are talking about when we differentiate sourcing and recruiting.

What is sourcing?

This becomes a really interesting question depending on whom you ask, what they do for a job and which size of company they work for.

The Wikipedia definition, which has had many edits from industry professionals, is as follows:

> Sourcing is a talent management discipline that is focused on the identification, assessment and engagement of skilled worker candidates through proactive recruiting techniques.[1]

I prefer the definition that Glen Cathey, a definite 'super sourcer' and Senior Vice President of talent strategy and innovation at KForce, uses:

> The proactive identification, engagement and assessment of talent focusing solely on non-applicants (typically passive talent) with the end goal of producing qualified, interested and available candidates.[2]

FIGURE 6.1 You can source people from many different places

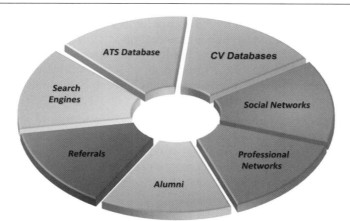

It tightens up the definition to include what many people have come to know sourcing via social media for – finding passive candidates. One thing that is true about sourcing is that, contrary to what some HR leaders believe, it is not an easy task and does require a certain set of skills. It is also important to note that the people aggregator search tools (mentioned in previous chapters) do not replace the sourcing function, although they can help, of course.

There are a variety of places that good sourcers can go to in order to find people, with some of the obvious areas shown in Figure 6.1.

Sourcing requires a certain set of skills that are not necessarily the same as recruiting, although there is significant crossover in the roles. During this, the term Boolean logic is used when discussing using search engines. Shannon Pritchett, Global Sourcing and Recruiting Specialist for ManpowerGroup Solutions RPO, shared her thoughts with me on this and describes it well:

> It's how sourcers speak to the search engines. The use of Boolean commands is the easiest way for sourcers to find information from billions of webpages. Though Boolean might be easy to use, it can be rather difficult to learn. Each search engine has its own unique set of Boolean commands. These commands are typically listed in the advanced search section. Once a sourcer has perfected their use of Boolean logic, they will be able to efficiently access more information from search engines.

So what is the difference between sourcing and recruiting?

This is very well explained by another 'super sourcer' and recruiter in the United States, Amybeth Quinn.[3] In a recent blog post she breaks down the two functions into their fundamental skills:[4]

- *Sourcing*:
  - Breaking this down into smaller sections, sourcing search fundamentals includes, but is not limited to, Boolean string creation; understanding internet taxonomy (being able to break down a URL and uncover hidden pages) – what Amybeth likes to call 'going down the rabbit hole' to follow a lead; and pulling together multiple information sources (both online and offline) to create a complete prospect profile.
  - Effective communication typically falls second behind search. However, it is a core skill that excellent sourcers must master in order to be successful. What good is uncovering the perfect person for a role if you cannot communicate with them effectively to pique their interest?
  - Scientific theory is not something you may associate with sourcing but, at its core, approaching a search using a sort-of scientific method will allow you to go through a trial-and-error process to test different approaches to your search, adjust when you are not finding what you need, and properly document your successes for your – and others' – future benefit.
- *Recruiting*: in addition to the sourcing fundamentals (a good recruiter must first be a good sourcer) a few basic fundamentals for recruiting include:
  - Project management: being able to craft an effective workflow – complete with timelines, responsibilities and assessments – is key to being an excellent recruiting partner to your clients. Without it, your recruiting process is a crap-shoot and you may as well attempt a career at cat herding.
  - Sales ability: even if you are working with a good sourcer who has already convinced a prospect that your role is perfect for them, a recruiter is still responsible for the 'purchase' – ie closing a candidate. At the heart of this is relationship development – becoming a trusted advisor to your candidates as well as your clients; after all, you are brokering that 'purchase' on both sides of the table, and the more both candidate and client trust you, the more effective you can be.

Common mastery areas for both sourcing and recruiting depend upon the industry in which you work. If you're going to focus on specific functions, you'd better learn your business – regardless of whether you are a sourcer or a recruiter. Does this now make sense to you? I like how Amybeth has usefully broken down the roles into 'real' role skills, rather than the usual narrative found on many job descriptions the world over.

Thus, now you understand what sourcing is all about, let us see how the 'super sourcers' go about searching for people on the different social networks.

Sourcing people on LinkedIn

LinkedIn is a subject that could justify a book on its own, so Katharine Robinson, who is a previous Sourcecon Grandmaster Sourcing Champion and is the founder of specialist consultancy Sourcing Hat in the UK has focused on some of the basics of LinkedIn that many people forget:[5]

LinkedIn is the world's largest online professional network, making it one of the most useful sources for finding and engaging with potential candidates. Before you start any sourcing activity, it is essential to have your LinkedIn profile up to scratch. For most people, their LinkedIn profile is the highest-ranking result for their name in a Google search. If you are reaching out to people via online messages or phone calls as part of your sourcing strategy, it is likely that those people will look you up and find your LinkedIn profile.

A basic LinkedIn account is free but there are multiple ways to upgrade your account. Before you look at these options, make sure that you are getting the most out of your basic account and know what you need from an upgraded option.

One of the best ways to make your basic LinkedIn account work better for you is to grow a powerful network. Your LinkedIn search results are heavily influenced by those directly connected to you – and their connections. By connecting to well-networked, relevant people you will find your LinkedIn network much improved. Joining LinkedIn groups is also a good way to add large numbers of relevant people to your searchable network. You can be a member of up to 50 groups: it is a good idea to maximize this opportunity in order to extend your network.

Upgrading your personal profile to become a premium member is often the most cost-effective option for individuals or a small team. A premium LinkedIn account will give you access to more search filters, the ability to view more profiles and an allocation of InMails each month.

The full LinkedIn Recruiter licences cost dramatically more but do offer many benefits. Those benefits include the ability to track the LinkedIn activity of your team, work collaboratively, use talent pipelining tools, access every profile on LinkedIn and send many more InMails. One of the most compelling advantages of upgrading to LinkedIn Recruiter licences is that all the activity relating to that licence is owned by the business that purchased the licence and that activity is kept separate from the individual's personal LinkedIn account. This protects both your business and employees from any awkward contact ownership issues when a recruiter decides to leave the business.

Searching on LinkedIn is deceptively easy. You put in keywords and you get back some relevant-looking candidates. However, it can quickly seem like you keep coming across the same profiles. Keyword variety is essential: think about all the different ways someone could describe the skills and experience you are looking for. Every keyword you enter rules out someone who has not described themselves in those exact terms. Boolean logic can be used to search LinkedIn too. Recruiters should be used to using Boolean for searching CV databases, but it is easy to forget that you can use it on LinkedIn too.

Many LinkedIn public profiles are indexed by search engines (such as Google and Bing), which means that you can search for LinkedIn profiles using the site search technique. Searching for LinkedIn profiles in this way can often help to uncover new profiles from outside of your network.

Once you have found a relevant candidate on LinkedIn you will want to get in touch with them. LinkedIn provides the InMail service for contacting its members, but I would urge you to check for alternative options before you use one. Does the profile list an e-mail address or phone number? Does the candidate link to a personal web page or another social media profile? All of these other avenues are free and show a much deeper understanding and interest from you.

When you do contact a candidate whom you found on LinkedIn, do let them know that this is where you learned about them and personalize the message to show that you read their profile. Adding a personal touch will greatly improve the likelihood that you will get a response.

How to source people on Twitter

Twitter is a social network that is packed with unstructured data, so sourcing needs a little planning and the right tools to find the people you need. Sarang Brahme, who is Global Head Social Recruiting at Cap Gemini, and a sourcing expert from India, shares his sourcing tips for Twitter:[6]

Twitter is one of the most underutilized tools for the recruitment community. In fact, even I started using it quite late in 2008; however now I am in 'addiction' phase. I am fully aware that not many recruiters will answer 'yes' to a question of have you had any hires from Twitter? My point of view is that Twitter is neither a structured database like LinkedIn nor is it an information database. Twitter is all about conversations, engagement, real-time listening and knowing the right people.

The first step for using Twitter is to follow the right people within your industry, domain, technology or region to listen and further engage them.

Here are five ways to use Twitter for recruitment:

1 Sourcing and job posting: with 284 million people on the platform, you can definitely try searching Twitter for your candidates.
Try searching with skills, location, job titles, target companies, etc. Followerwonk.com is the best tool I have come across to date.
You can also search Twitter's own interface and filter by 'People' tab. Keep your searches simple and short. Don't attempt to find candidates with all their skills – it is not a resume database. You can also post jobs with wise usage of hashtags. Use hashtags, skills and location, etc, while posting – but don't be a job-posting robot.
It should be only 20 per cent of what you say here.

2 Employer branding: use your employee's network to spread goodness about your talent brand across the target audience. Be interesting and authentic about what you say. Encourage your employees to post news, updates, internal events and activities through Twitter and build real-time influence about your talent brand. While you can run sponsored posts, paid contest – focus on organic growth and engagement.

3 Listening: right from asking if a certain company is good to join, to complaining about their bosses – everything happens on Twitter. Proactively listen to your internal/external talent about their views and comments. Also try to employ a formal listening engine to tap what people are saying about your company and use the information to develop your talent strategy.

4 Conversations/engagement: Twitter is very different from Facebook and LinkedIn. It is fast, real-time and conversational. If you are not conversing, you become obsolete on Twitter. Try to build conversations with your target talent, influencers and industry professionals. In the long run, it will help you to build larger connections and engagement. The amount of information you can gather on Twitter is beyond your limit to handle them. Use third-party tools such as Hootsuite to manage your social media efforts in a structured manner.

5 Learning: for me, this is one of the most important advantages of using Twitter. Over the years, by connecting with the right people in the industry, I have learnt so many new things. If you connect with the right people in the industry you can build a circle of social learning to learn/share best practices in the industry. Every conference has unique hashtags to learn from. TweetChats such as #TChat, BrandChat, #SourcingChat, #iHRChat are the primary source of learning for so many new professionals.

My mantra to every recruiter is simple: a) be active on Twitter; b) connect with the right people; c) share and learn; 4) be conversational and engage. I am sure that, as a recruiter, you will find Twitter a tool that you cannot live without.

How to source people on Facebook

Many people make the mistake that Facebook is a private social network and cannot be used for recruiting. Let me explain why Facebook is actually so good for recruitment sourcing.

Facebook has huge amounts of data across the entirety of its platform, from the biodata information you fill in when you join Facebook, to the friends you have, the pages you like, the content you post, the content you like, etc. They make *all* this data available for search, and they call this their Facebook Graph Search.

FIGURE 6.2   Facebook recruiting sample

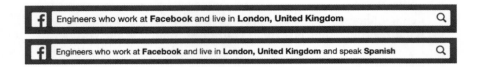

Unlike other social network searching, you cannot use a Boolean search string, as Facebook has created a unique search called Facebook Natural Language search. This is a little different and does take some getting used to in order to fully master it. As an example, Figure 6.2 shows you some searches you could do if you are recruiting for software engineers who work at Facebook and live in London.

There are many ways you can search for people based on the data that is on Facebook:

- People who work at *<company name>*.
- People who live in *<location>*.
- People who are from *<location>*.
- People who used to work at *<company>*.
- People who used to work at *<company>* and live in *<location>*.
- *<English graduates>* who live in *<location>* and speak *<language>*.
- People who graduated from university *<name>* after *<date>*.

To make it easier to search Facebook, there is an easy-to-use free tool created by Balazs Paroczay and Shane McCusker – **http://www.intel-sw.com/blog/facebook-search/** – shown in Figure 6.3.

Facebook Graph Search surprises many people with the depth of detail you can both search and filter on. While LinkedIn has more structured data, this type of Facebook searching allows you to find out different information on people, and it has four times as many people to search against.

Using Google+ to find people

Google+ is still an enigma for many recruiters, but it shouldn't be because it is such an excellent tool for recruiters to use to find people. When using Google+ to find people you first need to understand the many information points on which to base your search strings. Google+ has defined areas of data, as shown in Figure 6.4 on page 110.

FIGURE 6.3   Facebook search tool

The strange thing about Google+ is that we cannot fully utilize the normal Google search engine in the same way that we use it every day. It is not (currently) possible to use a full Boolean string within the Google+ search bar. You can use search operators, of course, but they are not nearly as functional as a Boolean string.

Your search results are broken down into six headers (Figure 6.5):

- Everything (the whole site).
- People and Pages (as highlighted in Figure 6.5).
- Communities.
- Google+ posts.
- Photos.
- More (Hangouts, Events, From Your Circles, From You, To You).

From a sourcing perspective, click on the 'People and Pages' tab. The results page is a scrolling grid of people profiles.

Another good way to search for people on Google+ is to search 'Communities'. These are a fantastic source of like-minded people – job titles, skills, industry, interests, alumni, locations, etc. Search for the types of

FIGURE 6.4   What can you search for on Google+?

FIGURE 6.5   Google+ search bar

communities that you would like to explore and search in the top search as before, but this time click on the 'Communities' tab.

The results will show a list of the communities, including the number of members and the number of posts. Figure 6.6 shows a community I set up called Recruiting With Google+, and as you can see it has 703 members currently. If you were looking for recruiters this would be a great place to start. These two methods are great, but the best way to search for people within Google+ is actually to perform an X-ray search (see the advice from Kelly Dingee, below) via Google. This way you can perform a good Boolean

FIGURE 6.6   Google+ communities

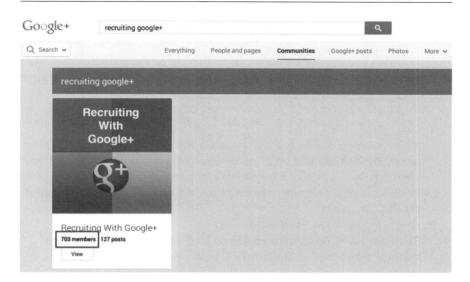

search and keep the results tight. For example, you could search for software developers who live in New York and work at Spotify like this:

site:plus.google.com inurl:about 'lives in new york' 'software engineer' 'works at spotify'.

The search looks for the phrases that Google+ uses to describe people in their bio – 'lives in New York' and 'works at Spotify' is how Google+ displays this information on the picture bio in a search result. The inurl:about is directing Google+ to search for content on the 'About' page, which is the lengthy bio page on the platform.

Google+ is a great social network for sourcing people – don't let people tell you otherwise.

How to use X-ray search for candidates

This is a search method that can be used on any website, including all the social media networks. The first professional sourcer I discovered many years ago, Kelly Dingee, is the Strategic Staffing Manager for Staffing Advisors in the United States. Her Twitter name sums her up – @SourcerKelly. Kelly shows how to use the different commands within a search engine in order to control and manipulate the search results to find people:[7]

The most important search operator for a recruiting professional to know is the 'site:' operator. Why is this command so important? It enables the user to see all pages of a website indexed by a search engine. All websites have a home, or a domain. Whether it is .com, .edu, .org or any of the additional domains released by ICANN in early 2014.[8] It is often referred to as an 'X-ray' because of its ability to create a structural view of a website. Digging into websites with this command will yield candidate names, organizational structure, profiles, lists and more.

The command 'site:' is a powerful one, not only because of the data it can yield but also because of its universal ability. It is always written as site: (lower case). Test it on Google, Bing, DuckDuckGo or the search engine flavour of the month and it yields a nice volume of results. Let's consider one way of using the command to extract information:

1 site:.org

When viewing results for any organization that resides on .org. they are in the hundreds of millions, and too many to reasonably view in a sitting. At this point, it is time to add additional keywords, phrases or additional search operators such as 'intitle:' or 'inurl:' to focus our results.

2 site:.org (intitle:staff OR inurl:staff)

Then we asked our search engine to look at websites on the .org domain with 'staff' in the title of the web page or in the URL (aka internet address). Our results should yield staff lists for a variety of organizations. We can continue to limit our results by adding locations, or specific job titles, or certifications.

3 site:.org (intitle:staff OR inurl:staff) 'cpa' 'dc' '202'

Now I've asked the search engine not only to search the .org top-level domain (considering all organizations) but also to find references to staff and on those staff pages to locate the acronym CPA, the abbreviation for Washington, DC, and the area code for Washington, DC. That narrows the results tremendously and focuses them in on a specific location and, more importantly, for CPAs (certified public accountants) working for organizations in the DC area.

4 In many cases, our clients will inquire if we can locate individuals at specific organizations. In that case, the 'site:' command can be used with a specific domain, like this:

site:iie.org

In this example, site:iie.org is scanning the domain for the Institute of International Education. It typically yields thousands of results. Again, team it with specific keywords or additional search operators such as 'intitle:' or 'inurl:' to focus results.

For example:

site:iie.org (intitle:staff OR inurl:staff) (vice OR vp)

This has the ability to yield key staff listed on iie.org and locate individuals with the title 'vp' or 'vice president'. If the search phrase (intitle:staff OR inurl:staff) had not returned results, it is possible to substitute similar terms such as management, leadership, team, bio, profile, etc, to yield information.

5   We could also use the 'site:' command on any number of social media sites to generate results for a targeted search:

> site:linkedin.com 'institute of international education' (vice OR vp)

This search views all the LinkedIn webpages indexed by our search engine and also looks for references to the Institute of International Education and for individuals with a reference to 'vp' or 'vice' on their page.

Additional tips

Test 'site:' with multiple domains (see ICANN for ideas) to get a feel for what the command can yield:

> site:.com site:.org site:.edu

Use keywords such as roster, attendee, management, leadership and so on to focus results with the 'intitle:' or 'inurl:' operators. Also try more advanced commands such as 'filetype:' to yield targeted results. Now that you know how to use these different searches you can apply the same search process across most of the social networks using the network URL as the search stem, eg site:twitter.com or site:pinterest.com.

Sourcing using video

This is an area that most people don't think of when considering sourcing, but Jim Stroud, Senior Director, RPO Recruitment Strategies and Support, Randstad Sourceright has been using it for years.[9] An innovator sourcing genius, Jim has also written *Resume Forensics: How to find free resumes and passive candidates on Google* (2011) and *Content is the New Sourcing: Strategies for attracting and engaging passive candidates* (2014). Jim tells us:

In the never-ending war for talent, it is assumed that it is becoming increasingly difficult to find people for your open positions. Actually, that is not true. With so many social networks, Boolean hacks and a proliferation of sourcing tools, finding people is becoming easier every day. The challenge is finding the right people, those star players who can literally work anywhere they want because, frankly, they have the skills that pay the bills. In fact, they are so good that they do not bother applying for jobs, which is why you cannot find them. It is difficult to locate them on niche websites and social networks. While they may be there networking with their peers, many of them have a disdain for recruiters and do not want to be contacted by them.

That said, how does a struggling recruiter, sourcer or talent acquisition manager get a better night's sleep? They do that by having an effective employment branding strategy. Quite simply, they have to present their company as not only a good place to work but *the* place to work. There are a number of ways to do that, but nothing delivers the goods quite like a well-placed video. For example, back in the day, I worked on Microsoft's international recruiting team sourcing software developers from all over the globe. The ultimate aim? To recruit them into our facility in Vancouver, aka 'Microsoft Canada Development Center'. To accomplish that feat, I created an inexpensive recruiting video and optimized it so that whenever someone did research on what it was like to work there, my video popped up. It worked like a charm.

I posted my video in 2008 and currently:

- It is a page one result on Google, Yahoo, Bing, AOL Search and Ask. (See for yourself. Look up 'Microsoft Canada Development Center' and my video will appear in the results, or a link to my video – 'Life at Microsoft's Canada Development Center' – will appear.)
- The video is still being viewed and shared. Check out this article from 2 May 2014: 'Microsoft Canada Excellence Centre to bring jobs to Vancouver' (**http://buff.ly/Zm1W9D**).

If I were to do the whole thing over again, it would be more difficult to get my video to rank now. Why? Spammers, hackers and competition for search engine placement has changed dramatically. Still, it is not impossible to score this type of free publicity for your company that can last (literally) for years. All you need is a bit of 'vseo magic' (VSEO stands for video search engine optimization or, in other words, how to get your recruiting video to the top of the search results every time).

While there are a plethora of things you must do to get your recruiting video in front of passive candidates you want to hire, for now, I'll share a few tips.

Watch time, social signals and video views

If you want your video to rank high on Google, it must get a lot of views, right? Not necessarily. If video A has 1,000 views and video B has 500 views, 10 comments and has been tweeted 50 times, then Google may actually show more love to video B. Why? Video B has had more social interaction, suggesting that it is a better-quality video. Video A might have had more views, but did people watch it all the way through? Maybe they watched for a few seconds and then went on to something else. If so, that is bad news for video A in terms of ranking. The bottom line is that viewers who watch your video all the way through and interact with it are better than those who witness your video but then leave half-way through.

Also, I mentioned how social interactions can affect your video ranking. The correct term is 'social signals'. Here is a short list of social signals that can boost your video ranking:

- tweets;
- Facebook shares;

- Facebook likes;
- comments on a video;
- Google +1s;
- LinkedIn mentions;
- video embeds;
- pins on Pinterest.

Keep in mind how people search

You might think that people search YouTube the same way they search Google. I thought that as well until I stumbled upon a tool called Keywordtool.io. This free online keyword research instrument uses Google Autocomplete to generate hundreds of relevant long-tail keywords. The search terms that are suggested are based on a number of different factors: one of them is how often users were searching for a particular term in the past.

So, why is this tool relevant for VSEO? It shows you Google suggestions for Google and on YouTube. For example, if I begin searching for 'recruiting video' on Google, the top three suggestions are: recruiting videos, recruiting volunteers and recruiting veterans. The top three suggestions on YouTube are: recruiting video (singular, not plural), recruiting video baseball and recruiting video softball. It is interesting, but why is it important?

When Google includes videos in its search results, more often than not it includes top-ranked videos on YouTube first. So, while you might be optimizing your videos to rank well on the Google search engine, it might be wiser to consider ranking on YouTube first.

Captions rock

An interesting feature is that you can caption your videos on YouTube. People can choose to click a button and read along with the action on your video if they so choose. This is wonderful for a couple of reasons. For one, it is great for VSEO. For example, Discovery Digital Networks captioned over 100 of its videos over eight YouTube channels and compared performance of those videos against ones that were not captioned. In the first 14 days it received a 13.48 per cent lift in views on those videos that were close-captioned. It also generated a lifetime increase of 7.32 per cent.[10] Another benefit? Close-captioning is great for getting the attention of people whose first language is not English (after all, according to YouTube's website, 80 per cent of YouTube traffic is from outside the United States).

The ultimate VSEO hack

No matter how clever your tactics, there is no getting around the obvious. *Your video has got to be good.* No one is going to watch or share something that does not keep their interest or solicit an emotional response – or is simply dull. Towards that end, I would like to suggest a few recruiting videos for the sake of inspiration:

Life at Shopify: YouTube (**http://buff.ly/1vHZCX0**).

At Twitter, The Future is You!: YouTube (**http://buff.ly/ZlTask**).

Lip Dub – Flagpole Sitta by Harvey Danger: Vimeo (**http://buff.ly/1vHZTZW**).

A Day in the Life of Rackspace – Get your Awesome On!: YouTube (**http://buff.ly/1vI05Zd**).

Life at Microsoft's Canada Development Center: YouTube (**http://buff.ly/ZlVbVq**).

Using images to source people

Social media networks are full of photos, so it makes sense to try and use them for sourcing, right? Oscar Mager, founder of Recruiting Essentials in the Netherlands, a multilingual specialist consultancy for international recruiting and talent sourcing, has developed this niche area of sourcing via images:[11]

In our increasingly visual world, images tell the story. Social networks have been early in recognizing this, together with the human urge to post, share, view, like and comment on photos. Images are the number one driver behind social network growth, helped by features that will make users upload even more photos, such as (auto) tagging and 'awesomizing' features.

The power of image search

In 2014, over 1.8 billion photos per day were uploaded and shared on platforms such as Whatsapp, Facebook, Instagram, Snapchat and Flickr. In late 2013, Yahoo already predicted the number of photos taken in 2014 to approach a staggering 1 trillion due to the selfie explosion. We are talking here about 'big data' sets.

To deal with this amount of pictures on the Facebook network, for example, Facebook alone has built three 'cold storage' data centres to store less popular or outdated photos. Each of their 16,000 square-foot data centres is able to hold an exabyte of data, or about 1 million PC hard drives. These images will not only be stored and indexed to easily retrieve them; from their computer vision systems backend – machine learning systems that have the power and intelligence to identify what is in an image, what a building looks like versus a face versus a landscape – social networks will use images to gain intelligence about what we are doing, who we are hanging out with and what our interests are. This is data that will most likely be of interest for their advertisers.

That's not all. More cameras, mobile phones, apps and social networks use GPS technology to exactly determine where photos have been taken. This information is stored in EXIF (exchangeable image file format) files, small data files embedded in images. Companies such as Facebook, Instagram, Google+ and Foursquare get access to this data as soon as their users post images to their networks. Have you ever wondered why social networks would like you to tag who is in your pictures?

A sourcer's gold mine

With all the information available in images, how valuable are images for talent sourcers? After all, sourcing is about finding people and gathering information about people. With the amount of photos that people have all over the internet, sometimes without even knowing of their existence, sourcers have access to an invaluable source of information. Images have become a sourcer's gold mine.

As a result of the popularity of using images, image search indeed can be a very powerful instrument for talent sourcing. A great starting point of image search is using avatar pictures or profile images. These images usually contain a person's face, and since most people have a habit of using one single image for different online profiles, it makes it relatively easy to find all the social networks a person is active in by simply conducting a search on the person's profile image. Interestingly, one of the benefits of using image search is that it can deliver more relevant results as opposed to only name searching. Especially for more common names, images prove better in identifying a unique person.

Google Images

One of the best ways to conduct an image search (as shown in Figure 6.7) is by using the reverse image search technique in Google Images. Most of the other examples of image search are variations of reverse image search.

There are basically four ways to search by image using Google Images:

- Drag and drop: drag and drop an image from the web or your computer into the search box on images.google.com.

FIGURE 6.7   Google Images search

- Upload an image: on images.google.com, click the camera icon, then select 'Upload an image'. Select the image you want to use to start your search.
- Copy and paste the image URL: right-click an image on the web to copy the URL. On images.google.com, click the camera icon, and 'Paste image URL'.
- Right-click an image on the web: to search by image even faster, download the Chrome extension (**https://chrome.google.com/ webstore/detail/dajedkncpodkggklbegccjpmnglmnflm?hl=en**) or the Firefox extension (**https://addons.mozilla.org/en-US/firefox/addon/ search-by-image-by-google/**). With the extension installed, simply right-click any image on the web directly and select 'Search Google with this image' to initiate the image search.

If you are confused, these techniques are also explained in a video.[12]

Both Chrome and Firefox browsers have multiple reverse image search plugins and extensions available. To install these visit their web stores and search for 'image search' in the search bar. Most of these plugins are based on Google's image search technology. It can be worth trying different tools in different browsers though, as search results may vary.

Applying either of these techniques to an image containing a person's face will result in Google finding similar pictures of that person and redirecting you to the profiles containing the pictures. An additional step to take in this search is to click on the 'Find other sizes of this image' link(s) next to the initial search result in order to find more results with the same image, only in different sizes (Figure 6.8).

Social networks all have set their specific image dimensions for the different parts of the social network where profile images are being used and all image sizes are stored separately, making it more convenient to find multiple online profiles of a person by using a single image.

Once a search engine is able not only to identify similar images, but also is able to establish the name of the person in the image, search results get even more interesting and often show other images of the same person. These results usually contain images of other social profiles connected to the same person, which subsequently can be used to explore further by right-clicking the image using a reverse image search plugin again.

FIGURE 6.8   Search to find other sizes of the same image

Image size:
200 × 200

Find other sizes of this image:
All sizes - Small

The same technique can be applied not only to profile images, but to any other image that contains a face. Think of images on company introduction pages (meet the team), event pictures, pictures used for online check-ins on Foursquare, photo sharing communities such as Flickr, blogger profiles and much more.

Uploading an existing image with a person's face to one of the search engines is just one method. Alternatively, interesting results can be obtained by cropping a person's face from a larger image of a group of people and uploading the cropped image to the search engine.

Google is not the only search engine offering image search technology. Some other search engines that have image search functionality enabled are worth exploring for image search purposes:

- **https://images.search.yahoo.com/**
- **https://www.bing.com/images**
- **http://yandex.com/images/** (Russia)
- **http://image.baidu.com/** (China)

Other search engines are dedicated to reverse image search, some of which offer more advanced image search utilities:

- **http://tineye.com/**
- **http://www.imageraider.com/**
- **http://karmadecay.com/**
- **http://imgops.com/**

The future of visual sourcing

In the near future, image search technology will become far more advanced, as social networks and search engines will benefit from facial recognition technology becoming more accurate. Most of this technology is already available and is used by governments to prevent crime, but commercial use is still very much restricted by privacy regulations. The major breakthrough of image search for talent sourcing will most likely be wearable devices having facial recognition technology enabled and linking this to all image data sets and social networks to allow visual sourcing on-the-go.

Sourcing senior candidates

To prove to you that sourcing via social media is not just restricted to low- to mid-level roles, Shannon Pritchett, Global Sourcing and Recruiting Specialist for ManpowerGroup Solutions RPO in the United States, shares her considerable sourcing wisdom and shows you how to source senior candidates:[13]

Today, almost everyone is online. According to the internet world statistics, 7 billion people have access to internet services. Of those 7 billion, another 1.3 billion people belong to at least one social or professional media site. With statistics this high, a sourcer can fill most positions through talent actively sourced online.

Search engines have been a favourite tool for sourcers to use to hunt passive talent. There are many search engines available for sourcers to use, such as Google, Ask, Baidu, Bing, Blekko, DuckDuckGo, Exalead and Yandex. A sourcer does not need to use eight different search engines to fill a position, but each search engine indexes a different set of results. Knowing this, a sourcer can use multiple search engines to retrieve more webpages and more candidate information.

There is no doubt that almost everyone is online. You can fill almost any positions using advanced internet sourcing techniques. Most often, sourcers will use advanced internet sourcing techniques to focus on placing senior talent. Senior positions can be difficult to fill. You normally don't receive hundreds of applications for a senior position, as you would a more entry level, or blue-collar position. Additionally, most organizations like to attract passive talent. In doing so, a sourcer will have to be creative to find a perfect match.

Senior professionals tend to be listed more on the web than most other positions. As the seniority of the position increases, the talent pool narrows. However, compared to other positions, senior talent is often mentioned on a variety of different webpages, such as company webpages, speaking at events, attending conferences, contributing to an article and even sourcing their social or professional networking page. Through the use of search engines and Boolean logic, sourcers can quickly target and locate these senior individuals.

In combination with Boolean commands, a sourcer can use relatable keywords to target senior talent. A sourcer will first typically target resumes, CVs, portfolios and other online profiles of senior talent. The use of the 'intitle:' and 'inurl:' commands allow a sourcer to target specific keywords in the title field and URL address of a web page. Though rather long in length, this is a typical search used by sourcers to find online profiles:

> intitle:resume OR inurl:resume OR intitle:cv OR inurl:cv OR intitle:vitae OR inurl:vitae OR intitle:portfolio OR inurl:portfolio OR intitle:profile OR inurl:profile OR intitle:'about me' OR inurl:'about me'.

A sourcer will also use the popular site Boolean command to target many social and professional networking sites. This command is a favourite for many sources to quickly search for profiles on LinkedIn.

Using site:linkedin.com will allow the search to retrieve results only from LinkedIn. It is also an easy way to access over 300 million professionals on that site. Lastly, a sourcer can also look for a list of employees of an organization, or perhaps an online roster to also locate senior talent:

intitle:team OR inurl:team OR intitle:roster OR inurl:roster OR intitle:people OR inurl:people OR intitle:speakers OR inurl:speakers OR intitle:attendees OR inurl:attendees OR intitle:employees OR inurl:employees.

It is important for sourcers to remember that not every senior professional has their resume or CV online, or even a presence on LinkedIn. Expanding the search to focus on targeted web pages, paired with a job title and key-words related to the position can sometimes provide just as great a result. Through perfecting advanced internet sourcing techniques, a sourcer's opportunity to find senior talent is almost limitless.

International sourcing

Martin Lee, Vice President, Head of Sourcing and Research, EMEA and APAC at Kelly Services, is a sourcing genius and has shared his knowledge about sourcing people internationally, and the challenges that this brings:[14]

Whilst it is true that social media and the internet have removed many of the barriers for sourcers, finding candidates overseas still gives rise to additional challenges in an extremely competitive market. In general it is considered to be better for people to be based in the location they are trying to recruit from, due to language and cultural knowledge. However, more sourcers these days find themselves saddled with the challenge of being in a different country to the one they are searching for talent in. Tools such as Google translate make this possible. There is no reason why a great sourcer cannot work on any job anywhere in the world.

There are three obvious ways to tackle the search:

1 Look for people in the area you are recruiting for.

2 Search for people elsewhere who are suitable and eligible to work in that location. When you see companies sponsoring visas, you know they are struggling to recruit – because this is costly and time consuming.

3 Find people who are originally from that area but now working elsewhere – with a view to bringing them back 'home'.

When we search ATSs, databases, job boards, social media and the internet, we do so with keywords. We interpret a job description and create a search, but every time we add a keyword we exclude people from our results. For example, if we were to search for 'sales executive' or 'new business', we would not find people who call themselves an 'account manager', so every search result is different.

The first technique, therefore, is to find target companies with people doing the same job so that you don't have to rely on being accurate with your keyword searches. As you search internationally, you should always use a variety of language options in order to give a broad set of results.

If your search focuses on looking for talent from one country to bring into another then you have to find the most probable reasons that a candidate would change location, in addition to matching the position to their skills. Therein lies the power of big data, tools and technique.

For instance, if you were to search for companies in the semiconductor market in São Paulo, Brazil, an English word search would generate just one result. If you searched using the equivalent words translated into Portuguese then the results would tell a different story (Figure 6.9).

As shown in Figure 6.9, we now have a list of places to hunt for the perfect candidate, using various social media platforms and websites specific to the countries we are searching in. Using Spanish or other languages spoken in Brazil could yield even more results. Interrupting words simply using Google translate can give good results, but it is good to consider how a native speaker would say or write details about themselves online.

Always call on native speakers to help when searching, if you have people in your business that can do so then get their help. If not, there are plenty of cost-efficient resources available; it is just a matter of conducting another search.

As a rule, people who originate from the location you are recruiting for, but who now work elsewhere, have a higher probability of being interested in your role than others not from that area, due to knowledge of the area, family and perhaps a desire to return home.

There are areas of social media sites that help us to find these people. LinkedIn has groups relating to people's nationality where we can search. Additionally, Alumni Search lets us use long Boolean strings to filter by university, school or college attended in relation to where they work now. Facebook Graph search also allows you to tailor your search in this way with its additional filters of 'Current City' versus 'Hometown'.

Twitter is known for having a lot of 'noise'; however, when you have something specific you are searching for, it can be a great resource. There are many recruiters and agencies that specialize in overseas jobs and – as Twitter is free – they advertise them there. We can see their followers but also people showing an interest in their vacancies. Hootsuite is also a great tool to use for this.

Boolean strings also give us ways to find these people. For example, if you are searching for French people working in London with this basic string *site:fr.linkedin.com 'location * London'*.

Here's the checklist:

- Where do the candidates you are looking for go online?
- How will their information appear online?
- Which language or terminology would they use?
- How should I search for them?

FIGURE 6.9 Search map

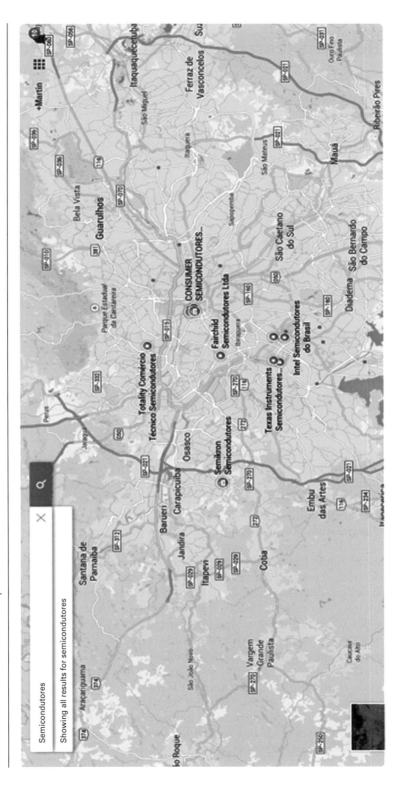

If Boolean searching is just too much for you

Jonathan Campbell, CEO of Social Talent, a recruitment sourcing and training company, and his team have created a tool that will save you the effort of constructing your own Boolean strings.[15] It is called SourceHub (shown in Figure 6.10) and it requires you to put in the job title, skills and city and then the tool will build the search strings on the social platforms you need to search on, with all the required synonyms.

FIGURE 6.10   SourceHub

Campbell believes that the 'research' part of sourcing will soon be automated to such a high degree that constructing a Boolean string and then searching in 10 different places to build a shortlist of candidates will be a thing of the past.

SourceHub (**https://source.socialtalent.co/**) is aimed at anyone who wants to find people and wants to make sure they are finding everyone, in as little time as possible. It is a free tool and carries provenance as it was designed and created by recruiters, for recruiters.

Social Talent has trained thousands of recruiters and sourcers all over the world and, therefore, Campbell was well placed to answer my question: what can recruiters/sourcers do to stay ahead of their competition? 'Embrace technology', he replied. 'Don't see yourself as a sourcer, see yourself as a provider of excellent talent and be prepared to move up that food chain, learning more "value added" techniques such as candidate engagement, employer branding and digital marketing. These are the skills of the future recruiter and it will be a long time before they are automated.'

Aside from all these great sourcers mentioned in this chapter, there are two people I want to mention whom I have learned much from over the last few years with regards to sourcing techniques, and they are Glen Cathey[16] and Irina Shamaeva.[17] If you are serious about sourcing then make sure you take a look at their websites for great Boolean sourcing advice.

Summary

For anyone in recruitment this chapter is a gold mine of information for sourcing people online. With the new skills you have learnt from some of the world's best sourcing professionals, you are now able to use search engines or any of the main social networks to identify and source potential new candidates. Some key points to consider from this chapter:

- While LinkedIn is the world's biggest professional network and is used by every recruiter, remember it is not the only social network to source talent from. Not everyone you are looking to find is on that platform.

- Sourcing is not an exact science, and as such needs practice and persistence in order to become very effective at using it. The more time you invest in using it, the better you will become, and the more people you will find.

- Don't make any assumptions on which social networks are best. The only way to find out is to start using them and find out where your target audience actually is.

Notes

1 https://en.wikipedia.org/wiki/Sourcing_%28personnel%29.
2 http://booleanblackbelt.com/2014/01/what-is-sourcing-i-propose-a-new-universal-definition/.
3 http://www.linkedin.com/in/researchgoddess.
4 http://www.researchgoddess.com/2014/08/properly-equipping-future-generation-excellent-sourcers/.
5 https://www.linkedin.com/in/katharinerobinson.
6 https://www.linkedin.com/in/sarangbrahme.
7 https://www.linkedin.com/in/kellydingeeb.
8 http://newgtlds.icann.org/en/.
9 https://www.linkedin.com/in/jimstroud.
10 Read all about it here: Adding Closed Captions to YouTube Videos Increases Views [Online] http://buff.ly/1vHYJhl.
11 https://www.linkedin.com/in/oscarmager.
12 https://www.youtube.com/watch?v=t99BfDnBZcI.
13 http://about.me/sourcingshannonb.
14 https://www.linkedin.com/in/martinjlee.
15 http://www.socialtalent.co/; https://www.linkedin.com/in/johnnycampbell.
16 http://booleanblackbelt.com/.
17 http://booleanstrings.com/.

Building your employer brand

The employer brand has become a very important area for employers, given the transparent and viral nature of social media. Whether you like it or not, your brand is potentially exposed 24/7 across all the social channels, even if you do not actually have a presence on them. With the ever-present skills shortages, having a good employer brand (perceived or real) is crucial for a company to enable them to hire and retain the talent they need.

The growth of visual media on sites such as LinkedIn, YouTube, Facebook, Instagram and Pinterest has really helped companies to tell their story to prospective candidates and to show them the benefits of working there. The best stories are from the employees themselves, and whether they are stand-alone videos or stories attached to photos, they always prove to be very effective in showing the real side to the company.

A good example of this is the Pinterest page 'Work at Campbell Arnott's', shown in Figure 7.1.[1] They have captured content about their employees and their stories from other social media networks they are using for recruiting, and brought it all together on one Pinterest board. It works well for companies, having all the content in one visible place.

In earlier chapters I have covered the different social networks and looked at examples where companies are using them for promoting their employment brands. In this chapter I focus on how your company can use social media to help you develop your brand if you don't have access to all the great self-generated content that the bigger brands have. I am referring to recruitment content marketing, and it is something that is effective for both companies with little time or resource to create large amounts of their own content, as well as companies with larger budgets.

Across most industries and sectors, candidates now have multiple choices of employers to choose from when they are looking for that next opportunity. Therefore, having a positive employer brand will help your company to:

- attract new candidates;
- increase employee engagement;
- be seen as an employer of choice;
- reduce your recruitment costs;
- increase staff retention.

FIGURE 7.1 Pinterest page for Campbell Arnott's

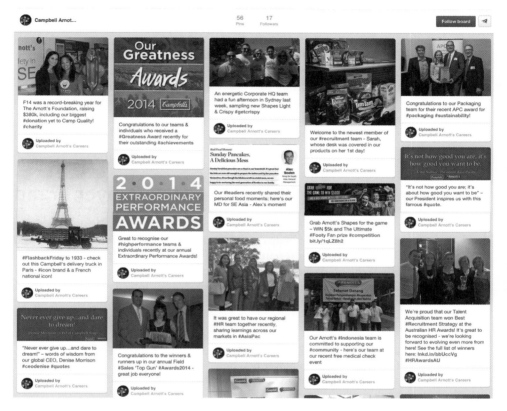

This may well seem obvious to you, but from my experiences many companies, particularly non-enterprise-sized organizations, are still struggling to comprehend the importance that a good employer brand has on recruitment success.

For example, LinkedIn produced a list of North America's in-demand employers for 2014:[2]

1 Google.

2 Apple.

3 Amazon.

4 Facebook.

5 Salesforce.

6 The Walt Disney Company.

7 Nike.

8 Microsoft.

9 McKinsey & Co.

10 PepsiCo.

Who wouldn't want to work for any of these companies? They all have tremendously strong employer brands and, unsurprisingly, they all successfully attract top talent. But what about the thousands of companies out there in the market – specifically the SMEs – who don't have the luxury of this level of brand behind them? They will still have great roles available with great people leading the companies. It doesn't make them poor employers, the problem may simply be that they have no employer brand and therefore may not be as attractive to jobseekers, because they are not visible enough in their sectors.

We therefore need to look past the employer brand and break this down further.

How to further enhance the employer brand

There needs to be an additional definition to be added when we are discussing employer branding, which helps to explain the benefits to the employees and potential employees at different stages of the candidate attraction process. This is called the employee value proposition (EVP).

Brett Minchington, CEO of Employer Brand International, describes them both:

> An employer brand is the image of your organisation as a 'great place to work' in the mind of current employees and key stakeholders in the external market (active and passive candidates, clients, customers and other key stakeholders). The art and science of employer branding is therefore concerned with the attraction, engagement and retention initiatives targeted at enhancing your company's employer brand.[3]

Taking this a stage further, you need to be able to identify what your organization has to offer employees – both existing and new. Minchington goes on to define what he calls the employer value proposition (EVP):

> An EVP is a set of associations and offerings provided by an organisation in return for the skills, capabilities and experiences an employee brings to the organisation. The EVP is an employee-centred approach that is aligned to existing, integrated workforce planning strategies because it has been informed by existing employees and the external target audience.

For companies to fully immerse themselves in the EVP they will need to integrate social media into their career sites and their recruiting activities, allowing them to listen and participate in the conversations in and around their brand with their prospective employees and interested applicants.

This presents problems for many companies:

- Social media is real-time, engaging, interactive, collaborative and mobile. The majority of existing career sites are static, boring, not intuitive and not mobile friendly. They do not best represent the employer brand at all.

- Online recruitment processes that sit behind career sites – the application tracking systems (ATS) – have not adapted well to the speed of change around social media and mobile. They are lengthy, clunky, overengineered and unfriendly towards candidates. While there have been significant improvements with the new breed of cloud-based ATS systems, the enterprise-level systems are still playing catch-up. As always in the enterprise, contracts are long, and change is slow, meaning this is a problem that will be around for a few years yet.
- Social media networks, while linked to company websites and career sites, are all stand-alone sites, with each one requiring detailed knowledge on how best to make it effective for recruiting. Very few recruiting departments or teams have fully dedicated social media resource.
- Social media is transparent and very fast to respond to any negativity around an employer brand. Prospective employees, when making that all-important decision whether to work for a company, are more commonly using sites such as Glassdoor.
- While there are many social 'listening tools' in the marketplace – at all levels of detail and cost – there is still a huge knowledge gap when it comes to HR and recruitment departments even knowing what is being said about their company, and subsequently their employer brand, online and on social media.
- Candidate expectations and awareness are changing due to the speed of change of technologies such as social media and mobile. They want richer content, easy-to-find and easy-to-navigate websites and social sites, easy-to-apply-for jobs and, of course, they want to be able to see it all on a mobile device.

The power, performance and perception of an employment brand will become either a key advantage or an inhibitor when it comes to future talent attraction and retention. It appears as though HR and talent directors are finally grasping the concept that social media will be integral to whether they hire and retain the required number of employees in the future.

A great example of a company doing this successfully is Earls restaurant chain in Canada.

CASE STUDY   How Earls use their employer brand to recruit

Earls is a company that has no recruiting team, no ATS and no HR department and yet still manages to hire hundreds of motivated employees every year for their 61 restaurants across Canada and the United States – there must be a really good reason why.

FIGURE 7.2   Earls wants you!

Earls restaurant chain has been a successful family-owned business for 30 years; 85 per cent of their 7,000 employees are millennials, which are a workforce demographic that are notoriously difficult to keep happy.

Social media has become very effective for Earls as a recruiting tool, when other more traditional methods like job boards and Craigslist have failed to attract the right quality of applicants.

All the recruiting for the company is done at a local restaurant level, with applicants having to turn up and hand in a completed application form. They do not allow any online applications, and while they do advertise the types of roles and the jobs available on their very good career site, all you can do is download a form to fill in and take into the store from 2–5 pm. They also use the social channels to share them, as can be seen in Figure 7.2.

In today's world of online recruiting and fast-moving technologies, this may seem a strange way to hire people for *all* their vacancies. But actually it plays to the strength of Earls – its people and their great culture.

The strength of this great culture and engaged workforce (measured at 80 per cent engagement in a recent internal company survey, which also had an 82 per cent participation rate), is ideal for embracing social media as their primary recruitment channel. Social networks such as Facebook, Twitter, Instagram and

YouTube are perfect for Earls to show their culture, great food and drink, and what it is like to work there. They empowered their employees and gave them the platforms to talk about the brand they are proud to work for – and to celebrate their success. In simple terms, they gave all their employees a voice and encouraged them to use it.

When I spoke to Brenda Rigney, Vice President People Operations at Earls, she summed it up brilliantly: 'Our employees tell our story for us, whether that be face to face with our customers, or on the social networks. They are a huge part of our recruiting success. The majority of our roles in the business are promoted from within, so everyone who joins Earls has the opportunity to progress through the company, with the full support and training that we give them.'

Earls operate a complete non-judgemental policy, therefore helping to nurture their employees' use of sites such as Twitter, Instagram and Facebook. Their social media strategy is really quite simple – it is all about the brand, the employees and their stories. They have created a #myearls hashtag that they encourage everyone to use when posting content, and their social media branding is cleverly focused 'Earls Wants You', 'People Grow Here' and 'We've Got Soul'. And, of course, these are perfect for adding to images and sharing them across social media to constantly reinforce the recruiting messages, as shown in Figure 7.3 overleaf.

Earls uses the social networks as their recruiting channels, but they don't endlessly broadcast jobs, they let their employer brand (and their employees) do the work for them. They have promoted vacancies via a Facebook app and used PPC when launching a new restaurant in new locations, and they promote all the adverts on their career website **http://earlswantsyou.com/**, but you still have to apply locally for the job.

This strategy has been very successful, but could not have worked without the hard work that has created and maintained the culture and the brand at Earls, the sense of purpose they have given to their employees and the employee advocacy across social media.

Each year, Employer Brand International completes an Employer Branding Global Trends Study,[4] and in 2014 there was some encouraging data collected (based on 1,143 responses from 18 countries). It considers how companies are addressing the need to enhance their employer brands. As can be seen in Figure 7.4, social media is first, closely followed by the career site as things companies are focusing on to enhance their employer brand. Does this reflect what you are doing at your company to enhance your employer brand?

In striving for excellence, would your company take the bold step and actually be prepared to be assessed on its recruitment process, by the actual

FIGURE 7.3   Earls constantly reinforces its recruiting message

FIGURE 7.4   Which activities are you undertaking?

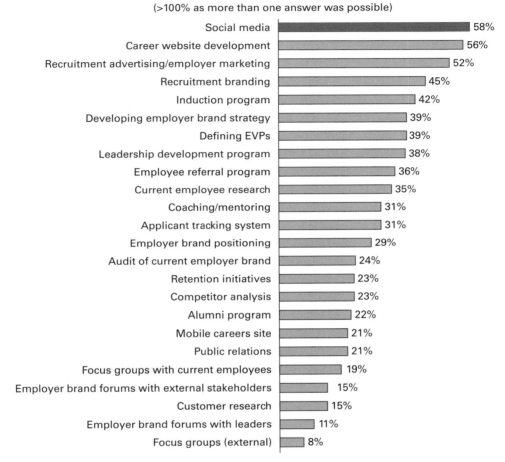

Which activities are you currently undertaking to enhance your employer brand?

(>100% as more than one answer was possible)

Activity	Percentage
Social media	58%
Career website development	56%
Recruitment advertising/employer marketing	52%
Recruitment branding	45%
Induction program	42%
Developing employer brand strategy	39%
Defining EVPs	39%
Leadership development program	38%
Employee referral program	36%
Current employee research	35%
Coaching/mentoring	31%
Applicant tracking system	31%
Employer brand positioning	29%
Audit of current employer brand	24%
Retention initiatives	23%
Competitor analysis	23%
Alumni program	22%
Mobile careers site	21%
Public relations	21%
Focus groups with current employees	19%
Employer brand forums with external stakeholders	15%
Customer research	15%
Employer brand forums with leaders	11%
Focus groups (external)	8%

SOURCE: Employer Brand International 2014 Employer Branding Global Trends Study

candidates themselves – both the successful applicants as well as the rejections along the way? Of course, the answer should be yes. Complete feedback is the only way forward in improvement.

In 2010, a non-profit organization called Talent Board was set up by three senior recruitment industry professionals, Gerry Crispin, Elaine Orler and Ed Newman, with the aim of helping to raise the standards of recruiting. The comparison metric (and benchmark) they chose to focus on was the candidate experience. This was an interesting metric to choose because it gives the real feedback on a company's recruitment process, not contrived statistics that companies often provide. The problem was that it required the candidates themselves to provide the essential feedback. Through a constantly evolving survey process they are now on their fourth year collecting this valuable data and providing the unique insight it gives.

The output of this annual programme is called The Candidate Experience Awards, also referred to as The CandEs. They are open to every company that wants to participate at no cost, and if they meet certain criteria by providing the level of data and transparency required then they can be included. The innovative part is that every company participating can receive a CandE award if they meet the minimum results criteria. Each year the outstanding companies are honoured. And with it all being transparent, the winning companies are very happy to share their best practices and their experiences.

The CandEs have now become the recruitment industry benchmark for good recruiting practices and provision of a good candidate experience. In 2014, North America completed its fourth year with the programme, with more than 170 companies registering and over 95,000 candidates responding with employer feedback. They are just now beginning to compile the data and analysis for their yearly report. It has also validated that interest in the candidate experience is a global phenomenon. The UK is just finishing its third annual award and benchmarking programme, and professionals in North America, Europe, Australia and New Zealand, South East Asia and South America have all expressed an interest in Talent Board's initiative for 2015. For more information on being involved in this benchmarking programme visit: **www.thecandes.org**.

There were some interesting findings from the 2013 CandE Awards, where Talent Board-evaluated survey responses from 46,000 candidates who applied to approximately 95 companies in the United States, were: a total of 59.5 per cent of candidates have some relationship with the employer at the onset, indicating a clear initial predisposition towards the employer and suggesting that positive association is the employer's to lose:

- Winners of the 2013 CandE Awards were more likely than non-winners to set expectations for the amount of time it would take to apply, provide details on privacy commitments, include screening questions customized to the job or job family and ask candidates for feedback on the process.

- There is room for improvement in regard to getting feedback from candidates, with just 31.2 per cent of organizations reporting that they ask candidates for such feedback, with only 14.8 per cent doing so routinely.

- Winners are also much more likely to have candidates who perceived that they were able to fully communicate their skills knowledge and experience to the employer through the application and, if they got further, through the interview process. Recruiting practices related to this concept of 'perceived fairness' had the highest correlation with a positive candidate experience.

- Nearly all candidates with a positive experience (96.9 per cent) would refer someone to apply again, while 33.2 per cent of those with a negative experience would still refer others, suggesting that some candidates will rise above their own experience and recognize the value that a job might offer to someone else.

Would you have the confidence and belief in your company's recruitment to enter these awards? From my experiences there are many companies that genuinely believe they have a good recruitment process, but they rarely consider the experience from the candidate's perspective. As more focus centres on areas such as candidate experience and employer branding, there is a real pressure on companies to examine their recruitment strategies, processes and social media activities around recruitment.

How can you enhance your employer brand by using recruitment content marketing and social media?

First, let's start by making sure you understand what I mean by recruitment content marketing. The definition by the Content Marketing Institute is described as:

> Content marketing is a marketing technique of creating and distributing valuable, relevant and consistent content to attract and acquire a clearly defined audience – with the objective of driving profitable customer action.

For recruitment content marketing the 'profitable customer action' is (ultimately) about driving people to a career website, and then for them to click on and apply for relevant jobs. Social media is one of the distribution mechanisms for this content.

As we discussed earlier in the chapter, having little or no 'real' employer brand can really impact the success of your recruitment activities. With so much competition in the marketplace for talent, anything that can be done to improve the chances of successful candidate engagement and subsequent applications becomes part of a candidate attraction strategy.

The purpose of recruitment content marketing is to attract and retain a targeted audience by consistently creating and curating relevant and valuable content, with the intention of enhancing the chances of this targeted audience applying for – or referring friends to – suitable jobs at an appropriate time. It is an ongoing process that needs to be integrated into your overall recruitment strategy.

Imagine for a moment that you are a recruiter who has taken the time to create and curate interesting and relevant content, and then shared it regularly with a specific target audience on one of the social media networks. A new job role has been given to you, and some of the perfect candidates are sitting within this target audience you have been cultivating. Being a good recruiter, you now want to pick up the phone to these potential candidates. You now have a big advantage because they:

- Already know who you are and what you do because they will have checked our your bio at some stage.
- Know that you are an expert in their sector/industry because of the insights you have added to the content you have created and shared.
- Know you already by reputation of someone who has been sharing great content in their sector/industry with them.
- Trust you.
- Know that your call will be worthwhile taking.

As a recruiter, you will definitely improve your chances of success in comparison to a cold call to the same audience.

If you are struggling to get your head around this, let me give you a simple analogy that demonstrates what I mean. Recruiting is often aligned to fishing. Imagine you are sitting in front of a large lake. Now think of this lake as a huge pool of talented people. You as the recruiter are going fishing. The successful fishermen are the ones who catch the best fish. To catch the best fish they first use ground bait (extra food) and scatter it in specific areas in the lake. They place this ground bait into the part of the lake they have identified as the area where the fish they want to catch are located. They regularly do this before they start fishing. They also carry on this extra baiting during their fishing. The fish are attracted to where this extra food is being continually directed, so it ensures there are more fish there more often. Then the fisherman puts the appropriate bait on the end of the hook and casts out to where he has been putting this ground bait. Guess what happens next? He catches all the fish he is trying to catch.

The unsuccessful fisherman turns up to the lake, picks a random place, places whatever bait he has to hand on his hook, casts out and sits waiting. He might catch a random fish, of course, but at the end of the day, he doesn't catch nearly as many.

Recruitment content marketing is similar. You identify the best place to find the right candidates and then, by sharing the right content consistently, you will attract the right people to you, therefore increasing your chances of capturing the better candidates for your jobs.

How to get started with recruitment content marketing

As with any new strategy you need to have a plan and structure to work to. Figure 7.5 shows a workflow that I use with companies. It is a combination

FIGURE 7.5 Recruitment content marketing workflow

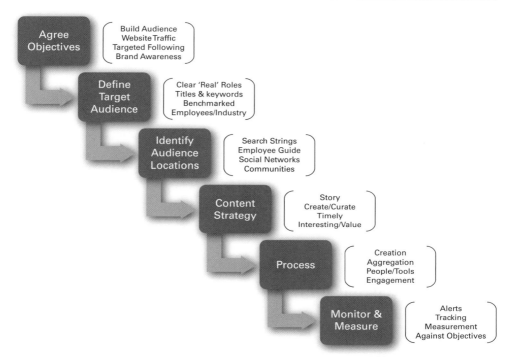

SOURCE: © Andy Headworth

of the specific needs of recruitment and a number of the core aspects of pure content marketing.

The workflow is broken down into six stages, and it is very important that you make sure you start at the beginning. Otherwise, you will not be able to measure the level of success against the original objectives you set.

Stage 1: agree objectives

Why are you going to do recruitment content marketing? What do you want to achieve by doing it? What results would you like to see? These are three straightforward questions that are often left unanswered by recruiters doing recruitment content marketing for the first time.

To be able to measure the effectiveness of your content marketing efforts, you need to set yourself some objectives before beginning. This will provide you with direction and a means of demonstrating success or failure.

These will be different for every company depending on different factors, and just to complicate things each social media network should have its own set of objectives, as they are all so different. Here are some examples objectives that you should be thinking about:

- Increase brand awareness.
- Build profile within a specific sector/industry.
- Build a targeted following by <date>.
- Increase connections/fans/likes by XX per cent.
- Increase traffic to career site from social media by XX per cent.
- Increase page views of blogs by XX per cent.
- Drive XX per cent more job applications from social media.
- Create six industry talent pools each with 100 people in it.
- Gain 1,000 new followers for your LinkedIn company page.
- Increase employee profile views on LinkedIn by 100 per cent.

Ideally these would be aligned to the objectives of your recruitment strategy, but they can be stand-alone objectives related to specific social media platforms.

Stage 2: define target audience

This part of the process should be similar to any direct sourcing activities you have in place. To target a specific audience of people you first need to know what they look like:

- Which job titles do they call themselves by?
- Are these job titles common with the rest of the industry? (This is important as many companies use weird and wonderful job titles that are unique to them, and are not ones commonly used by other companies.)
- What words/phrases do they use to describe their skills?
- What industry synonyms, keywords and buzzwords should you use?
- What company names or descriptive names for types of companies should you use?

A good example is from the recruitment industry itself: there are many versions of the title Talent Acquisition Manager. However, that isn't the word(s) a non-industry person would use to find a recruiter – they would search for keywords and phrases such as recruiter or recruitment or recruitment consultant.

As mentioned earlier, these are the types of information you would want to identify when placing adverts on job boards or building search strings for candidate sourcing methods.

Stage 3: identify audience locations

Now you have the essential information about what your target audience actually is, your task is to find out where they reside online. Finding people across the different social media platforms can be a real challenge because of the lack of unstructured data. The exceptions to the rule are sites such as LinkedIn, Viadeo and Xing, where performing detailed searches against company names, job titles, etc, delivers defined results.

Virtually every social media network has some form of bio or profile to identify the members and provide personal information about them. The challenge here lies with the fact that this is user-generated content, and as such can be incredibly varied. This is why the work in stage 2 is so important.

Not only can you search for the obvious personal information, but you can also search for the content that people are sharing on the different social networks themselves. You can do this by simply entering individual words or keywords into the search areas on the different social networks, or you can build Boolean search strings in order to save yourself time.

If you are skilled in creating Boolean strings then this will be easy, but if you have never used them before don't worry, it is very straightforward to get started. In simple terms, Boolean is a way of controlling the search results you get by using a series of triggers: AND, OR, ' ' and ( ). An example would be (staying with the talent acquisition manager theme): (recruiter OR 'recruitment' OR 'talent acquisition' OR 'recruiting') AND 'digital marketing'. This would look for people who have one of these common recruitment terms *and* digital marketing in their profiles and/or content that they post.

The good thing about Boolean is that most of the social networks will accept Boolean strings in their site search. So my advice is to create a spread-sheet containing different Boolean strings for different types of people you are searching for. Then apply these searches to a range of mainstream and niche social networks to find if your target audience is present on them.

Another good way to search the social networks is to search within groups, communities and lists that exist within sites such as LinkedIn, Google+ and Twitter. This will quickly identify larger numbers of your target audience and could save you a lot of time.

One obvious resource I haven't mentioned but which could be a tremendous asset for you in this task is your current employees (if employer) or candidates/contact/network (if you are a recruitment agency or recruitment process outsourcing, RPO). The people with the skills you are looking for will be similar to your existing employee base, so the simple answer is to ask them where they go online to chat and network with their peer groups. Human nature helps this greatly as we all tend to engage with like-minded people. For example, project managers or developers will naturally be in contact with other project managers and developers – sharing problems, solving problems or just investigating new methods and technologies.

Ask all your employees and don't take no for an answer when you ask them: this is valuable information that will be a great help to you.

Stage 4: content strategy

To a certain extent your content strategy will be dictated by the objectives you set out in stage 1. If you are looking to establish, develop or build out your employer brand, then you will need to ensure that you create your own content specific to your company. This should include all forms of content, including written text, photographs, images and video. As seen in Chapter 2, images, photographs and video are the most popular items shared across social media, and as such you need to ensure that your own content is a healthy mix of all of them.

I will not go into the actual creation of the content, as there is more than enough advice in that area from better qualified people than me. My go-to site for all things practical in social media is SocialMediaExaminer.com, and I would strongly suggest you take a look if you want some specific advice on using any of the social networks.

However, I would say that if you are going to create content, tell your company story and share great information, my advice would be to make sure you have a blog on which to do that. I am a little biased as I have been a blogger for eight years now, and use my blog (**http://sironaconsulting.com/blog**) to share content, ideas, presentations, videos, tips, advice and loads more. It has been a very successful source of clients as well, regularly generating conversations with new companies. Of course, I share my content across all the different social media networks.

I like to refer to blogs as content hubs because they have all of your content in one location; they sit on your domain, therefore increasing website traffic and search engine optimization; they are searchable at the same time as making it easy for people to make contact with you, while they are reading your content. Therefore, when creating a content strategy for social media – sharing articles, presentations, videos, etc from your own content hub are excellent for developing trust and credibility with your target audience.

A word of warning with regards to content that you choose to share across social media. It becomes very boring very quickly for all your fans, followers, connections and fellow group/community members if all you do is talk about your own company. The simple analogy to this is when you meet someone at a party or in a bar and strike up a conversation. If all that person does is talk about themselves continuously, then it isn't long before you've lost interest, made your excuses and walked away. The same thing happens in social media: if your content is not interesting, not relevant or does not provide any value to the reader then they are unlikely to follow you or connect with you.

A very effective way to make sure you don't just talk about your own company is to share great content from a wide variety of different sources. This is referred to as 'curating content'. This is a very good (and quick) way of establishing credibility within a specific industry or sector, without having to spend hours creating your own content.

The hardest part of curating content is finding all the great sources of blogs, articles, white papers, presentations, videos, etc that relate to your industry/sector. Do remember your target audience – so make sure you keep content sources on topic.

Stage 5: process

In recruitment one of the biggest challenges we have is time, and with the infinite amount of content online you need to use a tool that will enable you to find, read and share content quickly. Fortunately, there are many clever tools for identifying, indexing, reading and sharing (on social media) all different types of content. Some good curating tools (all have good free options) that you may recognize are:

- Feedly.com;
- Storify.com;
- List.ly;
- Scoop.it;
- Flipboard.com;
- Evernote.com.

These all work very well, but Feedly is my go-to tool for content curation because it does everything I need it to do: it can search for new content feeds; it allows me to manually add feeds; it categorizes content very well; it integrates with all my other online tools and sites, including all the social media networks; it has brilliant mobile apps; and, most importantly, it is very easy to use.

Here is how to use Feedly for easily finding and curating content to share with your audience:

1 Create a folder structure that mirrors the target audiences you want to reach. This makes it easy to pick out relevant suitable content quickly.

2 Search for interesting blogs and content feeds to add to these folders. In the top-right corner search for different subjects for which you want to find content. Click on the individual results for a preview of their content, and if you like it you simply add it under the category of your choice.

Every time that site posts new content, it immediately appears in your Feedly files.

3 Also search for blogs within search engines such as Google and Bing. Find the ones you like and manually add the RSS feed to Feedly by pasting it into the same search box as above.

4 When you have spent a little time adding feeds, you now have your own curated content library to select content from with which to share with your audience. Just to give you a guideline, you should be looking at adding 50–100 feeds to provide you with enough

interesting varied content to share. Not every post from all your feeds will be relevant (or good enough) for your audience.

5 When you want to share content, click on one of the categories you have chosen and you will see all the posts from all the feeds in that category in date order. This allows you to skim read them all in order to select the best and most suitable items to share. This method is quick and effective.

6 Feedly is integrated with many different social networks and online tools, and to share an item all you do is click on one of the icons directly above the post to share it with your network of choice.

This method is perfect to share individual pieces of content, but to make it really time-effective you need to *schedule* content to multiple social networks. This way, you can then schedule content at different times for hours, days or weeks in advance. Two such tools that are integrated with Feedly are BufferApp.com and Hootsuite. They both help you to understand the best times to post content for maximum reach, and provide you with analytics on the results. My recommendation would be Buffer because it is very easy to use in conjunction with Feedly, and the mobile/tablet experience is really excellent. As I said, my aim is to make this process as easy and efficient as possible for busy recruiters, and until we get the next piece of new technology these two tools work for me every time.

One question I always get asked is about frequency of posting across the different social networks, and how many times should recruiters tweet or update their accounts. There are no definite rules, but there are huge amounts of conflicting data on when to post – it just depends on which blog post you read at the time!

As always, with any marketing function (and social media is no different) you need to do your own testing and see what works for you and your audience. I would suggest that to start with you look to post several times a day on each of the platforms you are using, taking into account the times when your target audience is likely to be present. Obviously if you have an international audience you need to make sure you post content in their time zones, and remember early mornings, evenings and weekends as well as during the day when you are sharing your content.

Combining created and curated content

Ideally you should be looking at a mix of creating/sharing your own content combined with the curated content you have put together. A really important part of posting either forms of content is consistency. Regular posting each day, each week and each month will result in helping to develop a consistent and targeted following, as your audience get used to regularly associating you with quality content.

Rather than create content randomly, it would be advantageous to create a content calendar to help you plan all your content marketing. By having it in a calendar format it will help you visualize it and ensure you don't have gaps in the creation. It will also form a prompt to make sure you have content ready to post for the weeks ahead. This is particularly useful if there are multiple people who are tasked with creating different format types. You can also link the calendar to important industry events, which will allow you to maximize your marketing efforts.

As always, there are many ways that you can create and use a content calendar, and a quick search on Google will yield multiple free templates for you to use. Knowing the content that you have coming up on the calendar might also encourage you to identify and post similar curated content before and after your own content. However, I personally would not schedule curated content more than two weeks in advance, as it allows for you to stay current with the latest news, trends and industry changes.

Stage 6: monitor and measure

Monitoring

When you start to post content on social networks you want to ensure that you don't miss any opportunity for engagement with people that share, like or reply to your content. You need to set up correctly each social network to notify you and your team when this happens, in real time. There are two forms of notifications that prove to be the most effective – e-mails and push notifications on smartphones (as a recruiter is never far away from their phone):

- *Blog*: set up e-mail notifications to be alerted as soon as a comment is posted in order to allow for reply and/or release from moderation.
- *All social networks*: in 'Settings', set up e-mail notifications and permission for push notifications (for all users) for replies, mentions, comments and posts.
- *Any other brand, people, URL mentions online* (outside of the above): when people share your content online (without attributing it to you), mention your company name, brand, team members, etc, you should know that it is happening. While your company may employ the services of a social monitoring system for the core brand, it is unlikely that they will focus it on the recruitment or HR teams. You therefore need to track this as best you can (and, as always in recruitment and HR, with little or no budget).

    There are a number of tools that you can use to do this for little or no cost: Google Alerts, Mention.net, Hootsuite (Twitter), Tweetdeck (Twitter). They all work on the same premise – you provide the keywords, URL, names, etc that you want to track, and when these tools find an instance online where they have been mentioned they notify you immediately. This is extremely useful and again provides you with opportunities to engage with people who have become content advocates, by sharing your content or talking about you.

Measurement

Using the objectives you set out in stage 1, and tracking the results of your activities, you will be able to measure what ROI you are getting for your recruitment content marketing. You should be reviewing the results every month and making changes as required. Returning to the example objectives in Chapter 1, here are some ways that you would measure some of them:

- *Increase brand awareness*:
  - Blog: number of unique visits, return visits, search engine ranking.
  - Twitter: number of tweets about the brand, number of followers, tweets sentiment (positive/negative).
  - Facebook: number of likes, page visits, external posts.
  - LinkedIn: number of company page followers.
- *Build profile within a specific sector/industry*:
  - Blog: number of RSS/e-mail subscribers, comments, shares.
  - Twitter: analysis of followers/following (SocialBro.com), number of lists you are on, number of @replies.
  - Facebook: number of comments, likes on posts, user-generated content on page, post engagement.
  - LinkedIn: profile views by industry type, connection invites, search appearances.
  - Google+: number of circles you are in.
- *Increase connections/fans/likes by XX per cent*: measurement of connections, fans, likes, etc, between set dates.
- *Increase traffic to career site from social media by XX per cent*: using website analytics such as Google Analytics (free) to track career-site traffic visits from social media and mobile sites.
- *Drive XX per cent more job applications from social media*: some ATS systems will provide this data. Use specific tracking code from URL shortening tools such as Goo.gl or Bit.ly on links (compatible with Buffer and Hootsuite). At the very least, insert a self-serve question on application of source of brand/role awareness.

What you measure could, of course, vary for each campaign you create, but as long as you are clear on objectives and then measure them specifically you can then ascertain success or failure very clearly.

Summary

What story do you tell about your company? When you tell it do people ask you how they can join your company, or at least apply for a job there?

Whatever your answers to these questions, if you have done your homework and built your employment brand correctly, then your target audience should already know all about your company, your brand and, ideally, any career opportunities that might interest them. This chapter has shown you that you don't have to create endless amounts of content, and you can curate and share content that is interesting and relevant to your target audience. You may be surprised to find that you get more shares and engagement when you share content other than your own. The associations you create between your company and your target audience, when you share content that is either interesting or useful to them, is forged. They will then follow you on whatever platform(s) you are doing this. The trick then is to carry on the good work and keep the great content flowing.

There are some important things to remember from this chapter:

- Tell your story. Your employer brand is your story, your employees' story and the culture of your company.

- Don't be afraid to use different social media platforms to do this. Use the visual social networks to share your stories – they are shared more than the written word.

- Recruitment content marketing works – make sure you know your target audience – be clear on the objectives and understand the metrics for success.

Notes

1 http://www.pinterest.com/campbellarnotts/work-at-campbell-arnotts/.
2 Source: https://www.linkedin.com/indemand/.
3 B Minchington, *Your Employer Brand: Attract–engage–retain*, Torrensville, SA: Collective Learning Australia 2006.
4 2014 Employer Landing Global Trends Study Report.

Social media big data

Do your eyes glaze over when you hear people start talking about 'big data'? For me, it has become a 'catch-all' term that people use to describe anything that has significant amounts of data associated with it.[1] That could be social media data such as Twitter, which as of October 2014 processes 400 million tweets per day,[2] or something completely different such as the Tesco Clubcard loyalty programme that has 40+ million members and has a record of every single product they have purchased in their stores. There is no question that both represent big data, but surely big data only makes sense for recruiters and HR leaders if there is context to the data? Let me explain what I mean.

Gartner defines big data as: high-volume, high-velocity and high-variety information assets that demand cost-effective, innovative forms of information processing for enhanced insight and decision making.[3] The volume refers to the huge scale, the velocity refers to the speed that data is generated and streamed and the variety refers to the different types of data format – structured (traditional databases) and unstructured (e-mails, video, social media – updates, bios, posts, comments, etc).

This data has become vitally important to companies. More data may lead to more accurate analyses, which in turn may lead to better decision making. The confidence this brings could lead to significant business efficiencies, new strategies and new business opportunities.

But the reality with big data is not how 'big' it is: it is what you do with the data that makes the difference. This is even more relevant when you consider the data available to HR and recruitment departments, which allows for insights, analytics and the subsequent data-based decision making. At a conference in Amsterdam in 2014 Chris Hoyt, global talent and marketing leader at PepsiCo, summed it up well: 'Recruitment (big) data should be about the insights it gives not the actual reports themselves.'

For a recruiting, HR or talent leader the combination of big data and capable analytical tools can start to provide meaningful insights for a company such as:

- Where do our best employees come from? (Schools, universities, companies industries, etc.)
- What does the profile of our good employees look like? (Skills, background, personality, culture fit, etc.)

- Will video interviewing and assessments improve the quality of hire?
- How does our hiring process affect candidate retention?
- What is our future talent pipeline and where will the best talent be found?
- Which are the best candidate sources?

Earlier in the book I talked about the future of candidate sourcing across social media being people search aggregators. Rather than just explain big data, in this chapter I will show you five examples of how big data is now being used in HR and recruitment by different companies in different ways:

1 How LinkedIn uses their data to help recruiters and companies.

2 How one company is using candidate CV data to help them recruit based on culture fit.

3 How aggregated candidate searches across all the social media networks save you huge amounts of time.

4 How an SME used data to reduce hiring costs by two-thirds.

5 How big data has been used to dramatically improve recruitment reporting and decision making.

These are examples of some of the latest methods and tools in recruitment and HR (at time of writing) to use data in new and exciting ways, to help solicit important business decisions and/or make the job of a recruiter an easier one. Some of the client names have been removed at the request of the clients, while they transition these new methods and tools into the mainstream.

LinkedIn data visualization

LinkedIn is the world's largest professional network, with in excess of 200 million active monthly users. The huge difference between LinkedIn and all the other social networks is that the data is structured and, as such, can be accurately matched, searched and cross-referenced. This is why it is a fantastic tool for recruiters, because of the ability to interrogate the data (via search) in seemingly unlimited ways. In 2014 LinkedIn announced the complete redesign and rebuild of their search engine, with the new one being called Galene. It is a more powerful and intuitive search engine and one that will enable them to meet their vision.

The CEO of LinkedIn, Jeff Weiner, described the company's ultimate vision as aiming to have all of the global professional workforce (estimated by LinkedIn at 3 billion) on their platform (as of October 2014 they have 313 million members); to have all the companies these people work for listed on LinkedIn; all the jobs posted by these companies listed on LinkedIn; and all the world's colleges and universities that these people attended represented on their platform.

Then the plan is to enable recruiters to perform searches across all this data (*this really is big data territory*) to allow them to find exactly the individuals they want to identify in order to be able to hire them.

But it isn't just the recruiter that LinkedIn is planning to help – they want their hiring managers and senior HR/talent executives to gain a better insight into the talent pool that is relevant to them, in order to enable them to make accurate business decisions on their current and future hiring decisions. Figure 8.1 offers an example of what those search results and insights will look like within LinkedIn.

For all of you who have used LinkedIn in any detail, you will understand what a step this is for LinkedIn in aggregating the information and insights into an easier-to-understand dashboard. LinkedIn is fully tuned into the recruitment and HR industry and I am certainly looking forward to seeing the power of Galene develop and the insights it can produce over the next few years.

How to use CV data to recruit based on a culture fit

Data can be used in different ways to help companies at every stage in the recruitment process. Of course, how you manipulate and analyse the data is the crucial part.

Here is an example of a large retailer that was striving to solve a common problem in recruitment – reducing their time to hire. The challenge for this well-known retail brand leader wasn't a poor process, poor recruiters or attraction issue, it was the need to find candidates with the right culture fit for their company. This company's success is founded on its culture and core values, and therefore bringing new people into the organization who will fit into the culture is critical. This is what was taking the time. The identification of potentially suitable candidates, then assessments and multiple interview process were the main factors of the long time-to-hire metric.

They know the importance of understanding data and have a data scientist (and a behavioural psychologist) working within the company. But they still struggled with decreasing this time-to-hire metric, because the only data point they had was the application itself and the applicant's CV/resume.

They then engaged a company called eiTalent to help them. They look at written text (a CV, for example) and are able to provide predictive analysis based on language patterns correlated to the core value and culture markers of a specific company. In short, they can help companies to hire (and retain) people based on personality and culture fit.

It is fair to say that this retailer was initially sceptical that this approach could deliver statistically better results than they were currently getting. After a short amount of time understanding the core values and culture of this retailer, eiTalent were given four equal sets of 'cleansed' data from this

FIGURE 8.1 LinkedIn results

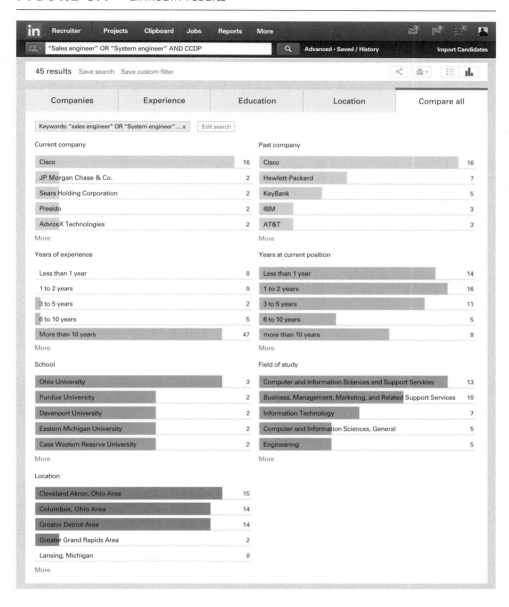

retailer as a blind test sample – group 1 consisted of those hired and promoted within a year, group 2 were those hired and fired within a year due to lack of culture fit, group 3 were those interviewed but not hired due to lack of culture fit and group 4 consisted of random resumes from a similar subset.

From this blind test the initial results got the retailer's attention. eiTalent's challenge was to predict which resumes fell into the hired/promoted, interviewed/not hired and hired/fired categories. They were able to predict with 84 per cent accuracy on the first pass, using only the their initial culture mapping.

The next stage was a real test based on specific groups (as opposed to a blind test). Once they had the key to which resumes were from each category, eiTalent was able to use that information to shift the algorithm and increase the accuracy to over 93 per cent. Additionally, by comparing the promoted versus fired resumes, eiTalent discovered a unique 'core values' signature and was able to build position-specific algorithm to help improve the company's hiring process even further.

The success of this project has led to the retailer changing their recruitment process by using eiTalent at the forefront of their recruitment process as well as considering using it for on boarding and ongoing employee assessment.

People search aggregators are changing the face of recruitment

People search aggregators are tools that allow employers or recruiters to search across multiple public social media sites at the same time, rather than sourcing them individually on Facebook, then LinkedIn, then Twitter, then Google+ or any other social network. They have been developed to allow a recruiter (for example) to search for specific skills, keywords, locations, companies and other parameters in order to find people who meet the required criteria across the many different search algorithms behind the social networks. And they work well.

Obviously, these come at a cost, and for many companies the ROI for using these types of tools is significant. The other thing to consider is that it gives the recruiters more time to engage with candidates and find the best hire rather than focusing much of their time on the sourcing aspect of their role.

Some of the most popular people aggregators today include Dice OpenWeb, TalentBin by Monster, Entelo, Gild, and Identified. The easiest way to explain them further is to show you what they can do. When you carry out a search on one of these people aggregators, as you will see in Figure 8.2 on the TalentBin example,[4] they have pulled data from many different sources; it also shows you multiple ways to get in contact with the person. This is a search that would take seconds on TalentBin but would take much longer if you were trying to find out all this information individually.

Dice OpenWeb also presents the results (shown in Figure 8.3 on p 152) with people's different social networks, as well as allowing the results to be further filtered to drill down the search to make it very specific.[5]

As you can see in the screenshots, these aggregators find people from many different sources, and organize the search results (or rank them) according to the focus of your search criteria. Some of the products then add in extra functions such as messaging/e-mailing in order to make it even easier to

FIGURE 8.2   TalentBin

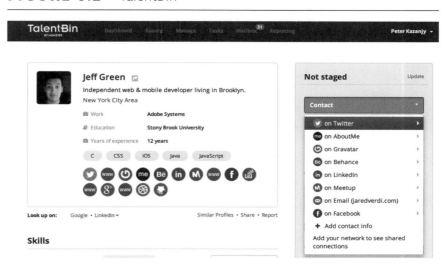

make effective time-saving. Some of them also offer integration with your ATS or CRM or, at the very least, the ability to export the search results to a spreadsheet via a CSV file. They are giving you more data on which to base your recruiting decisions.

These search aggregators are not yet fully global, and neither do they cover all the work professions – but they will in time. They have to-date focused on the industries and skills that have proved the hardest to search for over the last few years – technology, software developers, IT and sales and marketing professionals. But as their indexing becomes more complete these tools will be the future of identifying and sourcing candidates for companies and third-party recruiters.

Companies are now starting to take advantage of the proliferation of data to help them make decisions on talent strategy. This next example shows how an organization used many different data points to help them reduce their hiring costs.

CASE STUDY   How an SME used data to reduce hiring costs by two-thirds

A UK-based SME was experiencing 23 per cent top-line growth due to market demands. However, due to the lack of an infrastructure to support a seamless hiring process they experienced 18 months of recruitment problems, which positioned them in a reactive mode, rather than the proactive mode they sought to support their growth trajectory.

continues on p 153

FIGURE 8.3 Dice OpenWeb

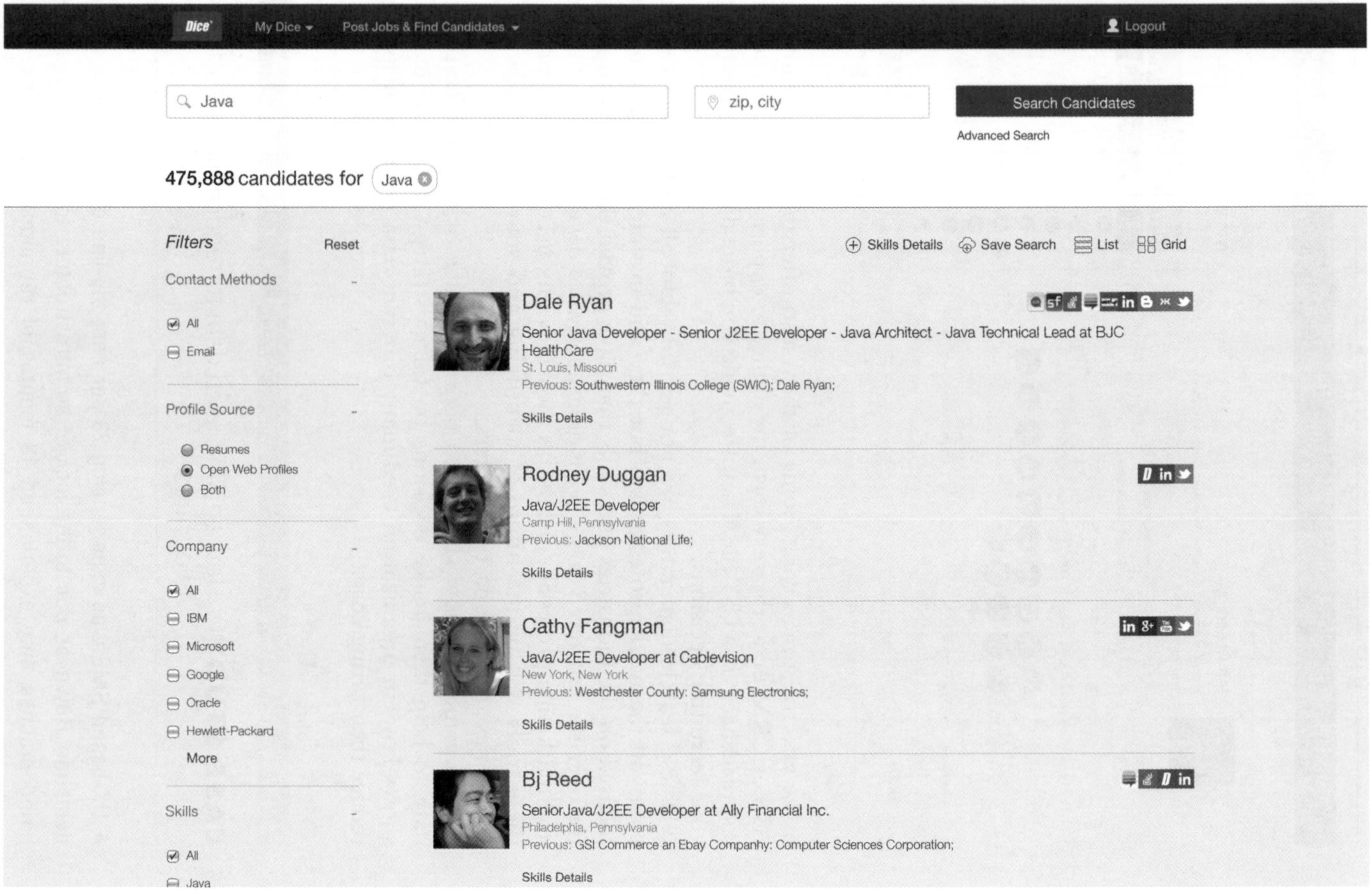

The high levels of executive frustration at the lack of progress to achieve consistency in talent sourcing, recruiting, interviewing and on boarding caused the company an increase in customer service disruption due to talent turnover and low quality hires.

They engaged Avancos – a global talent advisory firm that specializes in helping small and mid-sized businesses to accelerate, automate and improve talent acquisition by utilizing large data sources to help them make necessary business decisions.

Avancos approached the project from two angles: first they looked at the data and produced a talent intelligence report to better understand the talent market, trends, skills, compensation, competitors and market insights that would address immediate hiring needs, plus could be used to build a medium- and long-term attraction strategy (Figure 8.4).

Then they conducted an audit of the company's internal hiring processes, systems and interviewing tools set against a best practice benchmark. They identified the gaps between the current day and the targeted future talent objective, and then provided a road map and timeline to complete the project.

Immediately, the initial talent intelligence report revealed there was a customer perception gap of a talent-short market, yet the data said otherwise. It showed over 2,000 potential candidates within the company's defined parameters (skills, experience, qualifications) compared to the company's pool of 248 potential candidates. Furthermore, insights gained on the reality of talent pool available in the area confirmed that a lower local supply of candidates within a commutable radius was due to these candidates having been previous employees, already having been interviewed and rejected, or their not being open to a new opportunity.

FIGURE 8.4   Avancos map

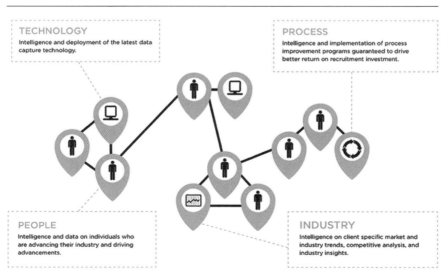

TECHNOLOGY
Intelligence and deployment of the latest data capture technology.

PROCESS
Intelligence and implementation of process improvement programs guaranteed to drive better return on recruitment investment.

PEOPLE
Intelligence and data on individuals who are advancing their industry and driving advancements.

INDUSTRY
Intelligence on client specific market and industry trends, competitive analysis, and industry insights.

Avancos recommended three options at this point:

1 Expand the radius and offer relocation assistance.
2 Discuss the merits/risks of regional locations to support their customers.
3 Change the job description to reflect the skills available locally.

The company chose to act on points 1 and 3 and within 30 days the company had a substantial pool of hireable candidates.

The audit also confirmed that in order to improve hiring outcomes, including accelerating hiring times, they needed to streamline the existing process and bring in tools to help provide consistency and accuracy when attracting talent. Avancos helped the company to define their roles into job families, create competencies, define who needed to be involved in the recruitment process and what role they should play, and created a process that provided a candidate experience that put them above their competitors.

The results meant that the company was able to identify talent in half the time, and accelerate interviews and on boarding from 180+ days to 45 days. The new approach improved outcome consistency, as demonstrated by a clear process in identifying, attracting and measuring talent (qualified candidate) against a benchmark. Equally important, the brand visibility, candidate experience and the overall quality of the talent pool improved, which resulted in reducing overall hiring costs by nearly two-thirds.

Big data, recruitment metrics and decision making

There is a huge amount of data available to HR and recruiting departments, all being fed in via different sources such as ATS, CRM, job boards, LinkedIn Recruiter, e-mail marketing, social media, referral schemes, job aggregators (such as Indeed), RPO, HRIS, etc. They all produce valid reporting but it is individual to that specific platform. The problem is that you actually need to pull in information from different data sources to be able to draw comparisons, and get valuable insights that you need to have in order to make the correct recruiting business decisions. Until recently this has been a challenge that required HR and recruitment leaders to produce multiple reports requiring manual entry of much of the data. In simple terms, there is no unified reporting hub.

This was a frustrating problem for Chris Hoyt, global talent and marketing leader at PepsiCo, who had this exact challenge but on a bigger scale than most, due to the truly global nature of PepsiCo. Through a conversation with one of their recruitment software providers, the journey of solving this big problem was started.

Broadbean has been providing recruitment solutions – job posting, social recruiting, referrals, CV search – and providing accurate reporting on them for 14 years, so they were well placed to help PepsiCo solve this big problem.

They created the big data analytics suite (BDAS), which (in very simple terms) takes data from *all* recruitment systems and puts them into a reporting suite. This then allows decision makers and stakeholders to create reports on a wide range of topics, and make informed business decisions.

BDAS links recruitment sourcing to the ATS and to the human resource information system (HRIS), helping to track ROI and measure the effectiveness of all your recruiters, wherever they are based. It has a custom analytics dashboard that provides faster access to key metrics, providing insight needed to make crucial decisions in terms of future investments, creating the ability to measure the revenue impact of recruitment practices.

Having seen BDAS I can certainly vouch that this product is a gamechanger with regards to recruitment metrics and reporting, and will help companies to measure accurately the effectiveness of their recruitment.

Reporting can be tailored, via this highly functional dashboard, for a wide variety of people in the recruitment process, as shown in Figure 8.5. The reports allow you to analyse both open and closed jobs, combining data from a wide range of sources, including career site, ATS, multi-posting system, web analytics and hiring manager surveys. You can report on groups of jobs (based on type or date range), or provide a comprehensive analysis of the activity for an individual job (Figure 8.6).

FIGURE 8.5   Big data analytics suite (BDAS)

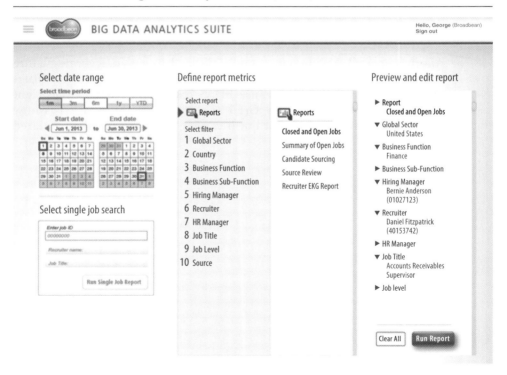

FIGURE 8.6   Summary of individual hired job

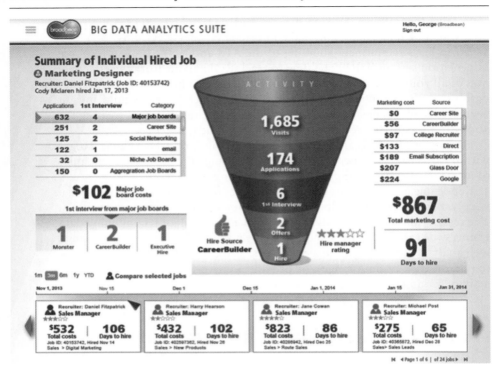

Another area where companies find it difficult to get an accurate picture from their data is the effectiveness – from advert to hire – of their different recruitment channels. Because BDAS takes data from sources right across this process, this Holy Grail of recruitment information is now readily at hand. Not only that but it can be sliced and diced as required (Figure 8.7).

FIGURE 8.7   Candidate source performance

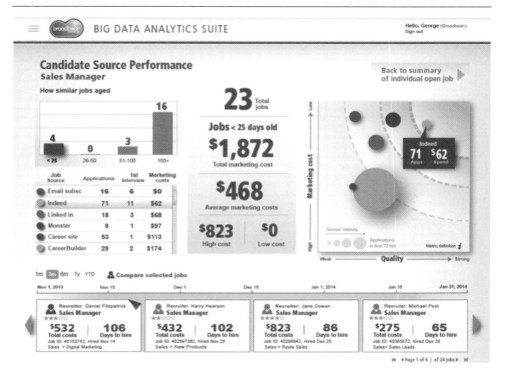

As well as enabling the business to better understand channel effectiveness and key hiring activity, BDAS also provides data to the HR and recruitment leaders to monitor the performance of the recruitment team – all measured against customizable KPIs (Figure 8.8).

As with all recruitment products on the marketplace, this new product can only work to its full potential if the groundwork is put in at the initial stages of the project, to define what is needed, and to ensure that all data inputs are fully understood.

Time will tell how PepsiCo learn from all the new reports they can now generate, but from what I have seen, the level of insights that BDAS provides will help them to make significant improvements in all aspects of their recruitment life cycle.

FIGURE 8.8   Recruiter EKG report

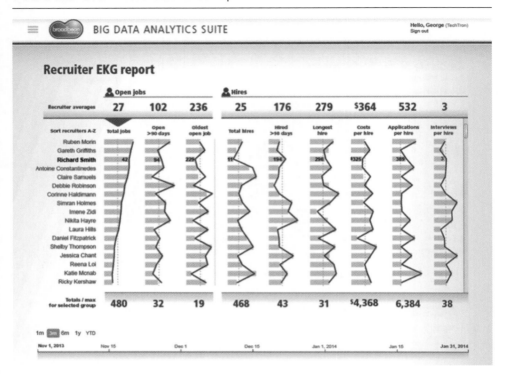

Summary

This chapter has shown that big data does have a place in recruitment. Everything we do in recruitment creates data that can be analysed, measured and dissected in many ways. The real problem with this data is knowing what to do with it and how to use it to help you make the correct recruiting and business decisions. As we see more products being developed to take advantage of the increasing amount of social data available to us, then more companies will base their decision making on fact rather than calculated guesses. Only then will they truly understand the implications of their decision making.

Recruitment data can be very valuable, but remember:

- Take the time to understand what the data you are looking at/using actually means to you in the context of what you are using it for. Too often you can get distracted with good-looking but ultimately meaningless information.

- When using platforms that provide you with huge amounts of information, take the time to learn how best to filter the results to your exact needs. LinkedIn is a good example of this – learn the parameters of the search results and the filters available, as they will give you more accurate results and save you time.

- If you are in a recruiting role, try some of the people search aggregators. They are here to stay in our industry, and if you are in the sectors/industries that are currently indexed by them, they may well become very valuable tools for you.

- While people search aggregators and such tools are superb, I want to remind you that they won't replace recruiters, but they will help them to work more efficiently.

Notes

1 See G Cathey, Analytics, Big Data & Moneyball HR/Recruiting for Dummies [Online] http://booleanblackbelt.com/2013/05/analytics-big-data-moneyball-hrrecruiting-for-dummies/.

2 http://www.dazeinfo.com/2014/08/16/twitter-inc-twtr-advertising-promoted-tweets-squaring-2014-us/.

3 http://www.gartner.com/it-glossary/big-data/.

4 https://www.talentbin.com.

5 http://www.dice.com/common/servlet/CommonController?op=15.

Establishing ROI   09

One of the first things that CEOs, managing directors and other senior executives will ask when confronted with a business case or proposal for the use of social media into their recruitment strategy is: 'What is the value to the business?'

It is their corporate responsibility to ask the question, but the answer is one that is not quite as exact as they may like. Of course it is possible to measure actions and activities during a recruitment process involving social media, through tracking links and the like. But social media is inherently about people and their different interactions with others, through chat, conversation and sharing, none of which are easy to fully track or measure.

For example, you share a new role on Twitter, someone then reads it on their iPhone and shares it with a friend in iMessage, who in turn e-mails it to their work colleague, who then does nothing with it for a month, then visits your website. It originated from your tweet, but how can this be tracked back to get the credit for it being from social media?

But that is not your answer when the CEO comes asking for the ROI from your department for using social media in your recruiting strategy. You will need to provide hard numbers in order to have any chance of your business case being signed off and agreed.

Before I help you to answer this specifically, there is one question you need to be able to answer truthfully, which will form the basis for you gaining a successful outcome to your request: what is the ROI of your existing recruitment methods for candidate attraction using job boards, recruitment agencies and recruitment advertising etc?

You only have two responses – a) you either know what it is exactly, or b) you have no idea.

From my experience, the latter is unfortunately the most common response I get from companies when I ask that question. They have an idea of what they believe to be the most effective channels, but have no data to back it up. Ultimately they have absolutely no idea what their existing ROI is, so how are they going to credibly predict an ROI for using social media in their recruitment strategy?

The companies that currently measure their recruitment effectively and can determine the ROI of the different aspects of their recruitment methods will be well placed to measure the levels of success of using different social media channels in their recruitment.

Thus, if your answer was 'b' then you first need to spend a little time understanding your existing metrics before you get too far involved with understanding your social media ROI.

When you consider how many different ways you could use the hundreds of different social media networks within your recruitment strategy, it is easy to understand how hard it can sometimes be to establish the value from using them. Many companies have made the mistake over the last few years of believing that simply by having a Facebook page, Twitter account or blog, and posting some content, they would naturally attract people to their 'new' social media activities. They succumbed to the common (yet flawed) well-known social media mantra of: 'If we build it they will come.'

For the large majority of these companies the audience never arrived, and these social media activities ended up being a short-lived one-way broadcast channel, destined to lie idle in the social media wasteland. There was no strategy or objectives in place to guide their activities, and therefore the only gauge of success was likely to be the number of followers, fans or likes. This in itself could have been a valid objective if that was indeed part of a strategy to increase the reach of the brand.

A big mistake people make when looking to start utilizing social media within their recruiting is to forget about the business objectives, instead focusing on the different social media tools, tactics and the networks, and allowing themselves to be sidetracked.

While it may be interesting and exciting to explore the myriad of 'shiny new' (and in many cases unproven) social media products, tools and software that offer to 'solve all your social media needs in one go', they are just not necessary to get started and will distract you from the all-important business objectives.

Getting started: objectives, targets and tactics

For companies who want to start using social media for recruitment I always start by asking four questions:

1 Why?
2 What are your objectives?
3 What do you want to achieve?
4 How are you going to do this?

This provides me with the answers as to whether they understand about social media, and how it could measure their recruitment activities.

Why do you want to start using social media for recruiting?

Understanding why you want to do it is fundamental for building out your objectives, setting targets and deciding on the tactics to be used. For example, common responses to this question are:

- We are not getting enough applications for our jobs on our career site, and we want to use social media to increase our visitors.
- We have been told that graduates are on Facebook, and want to use it to help us recruit our next graduate intake.
- We are spending too much money using recruitment agencies, and think social media can reduce that cost.

This 'why' question unfortunately proves difficult to answer for some people, with common answers being 'because everyone else is doing social media' and 'we felt we should be doing social media'.

What are your objectives for using social media for recruiting?

Without objectives, you have nothing to measure success or failure against, so these need to be clear and understood and, of course, ideally aligned with the business objectives. Some examples could be:

- Increasing the number of relevant job applications on a career site.
- Create graduate Facebook page in preparation for the next graduate recruitment campaign.
- Reduce the amount of money spent on recruitment agencies' fees by doing more direct candidate sourcing on social networks.

What do you want to achieve?

With objectives in place, you can start to add in the targets to measure effectiveness of the social media activities. Using the examples above:

- 500 click-throughs to the career site jobs from Twitter and Facebook in total.
- 300 page likes and 10 per cent engagement on the graduate Facebook page.
- Reduce agency spend by 20 per cent by sourcing candidates directly from LinkedIn, Twitter and Facebook.

How are you going to do this?

This is the final piece – the methods you use to achieve your objectives. So again with the same example:

- First establish where your audience is exactly, and the relevant keywords, job titles and locations they are in. Then using cost-effective pay per click (PPC) advertising on Facebook (including sponsored posts) and Twitter Cards, build a campaign to drive traffic to specific landing pages within the career site, ensuring the jobs are visible on the landing page.

- Research similar companies' graduate Facebook pages and the content they are posting in order to understand which types of content get the highest levels of engagement on their pages. Then you can try posting similar types of content on your graduate page. You can use the Facebook page 'Insights' tools to monitor five pages for free.

- First make sure you know exactly how much you are spending on recruitment agency fees and how much an average fee placement costs. Calculate 20 per cent of the total and divide it by the average fee. This is the number of successful hires you will need to source directly via LinkedIn, Twitter and Facebook (see Chapter 6 for how to do direct sourcing effectively).

Now you have understood the need for objectives, targets and tactics, there is another challenge to consider.

Different understanding of ROI within your structure

When starting to look at measuring ROI it is important to remember that ROI will mean different things to different levels within an organization. The hands-on users of social media will have different expectations of the ROI of their time than their managers and, ultimately, the CEO, who will be focused on the overall business ROI (see Figure 9.1).

FIGURE 9.1   Different ROI

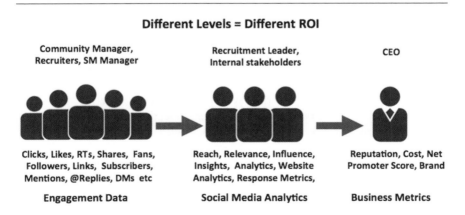

Different Levels = Different ROI

Community Manager, Recruiters, SM Manager	Recruitment Leader, Internal stakeholders	CEO

Clicks, Likes, RTs, Shares, Fans, Followers, Links, Subscribers, Mentions, @Replies, DMs etc	Reach, Relevance, Influence, Insights, Analytics, Website Analytics, Response Metrics,	Reputation, Cost, Net Promoter Score, Brand
Engagement Data	**Social Media Analytics**	**Business Metrics**

Day-to-day users are not interested in budgets and are more focused on the engagement data they generate from their own activities on social media. For these people, it is very much about the ROI of their time and the objectives and targets they have been set to achieve.

While the recruitment leaders and internal stakeholders are also concerned with the engagement data, they will also be looking at the analytics, and analysing the results in conjunction with other recruiting metrics from the website etc. The CEO is looking for a return on investing in your social media recruitment strategy, as well as the implications for the company's brand and reputation.

There are now many different tools to help with measuring all the different data, interactions, metrics and reach, and there are even some such as Klout and PeerIndex that are attempting to measure influence, although these are still, in my opinion, a work in progress (which is no surprise when trying to build an algorithm that understands what influences each of us to make an action).

From a recruiting perspective, when sharing jobs via the social media channels it is essential to add tracking code to the URL of the job link you share. Otherwise there will be no way of being able to specifically measure the applications that originated from social media. Fortunately many applicant tracking systems (ATS), online recruitment systems and job posting tools now automatically add unique tracking code to the job links they share online. Although it is worth checking the detail with your provider as the depth of accuracy may not always be to your requirements. If you don't have these tools in place and/or you want to track it yourself, then you can utilize the power of Google Analytics and then combine that with Hootsuite (Pro version).

You are able to add Google Analytics custom URL parameters to any URL shared on social networks that drives users back to your career site (or other website). You can then measure and track the performance of all your links via social media. By integrating this with Hootsuite you can then make this task a little easier to manage. Make sure you log all the content you share (including jobs) on a spreadsheet and number them. Place this number at the end of the relevant campaign title it matches. You will then be able to produce a report and show exactly the social media posts that drive the most traffic back to your career site or website. If you wish to understand this better then follow this process on this blog post: **http://blog.hootsuite.com/ track-social-media-campaigns/**.

There are numerous tools that will provide metrics for all the actual engagement data, including the individual social networks themselves. Facebook, LinkedIn, Pinterest, YouTube, Google+ and Twitter all provide you with analytics based on your activities. If you haven't had a look, they make for some interesting reading. Twitter is the latest social network to share your analytics with you, and if you haven't seen them before Figure 9.2 shows what they look like (using my Twitter account @andyheadworth).

FIGURE 9.2   Tweet activity graph

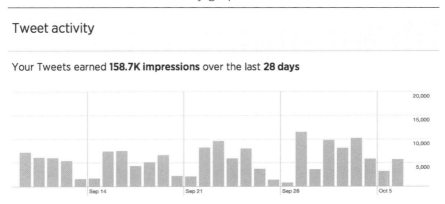

Tweet activity

Your Tweets earned **158.7K impressions** over the last **28 days**

In Figure 9.2 Twitter shows that during this 28-day period all my tweets for the month generated 158,700 impressions in people's Twitter feeds, meaning that number of people could potentially have read them.

Figure 9.3 shows an analysis of my Twitter followers, providing information on their interests, where they are based, their gender and other common Twitter users they follow.

FIGURE 9.3   Twitter analytics

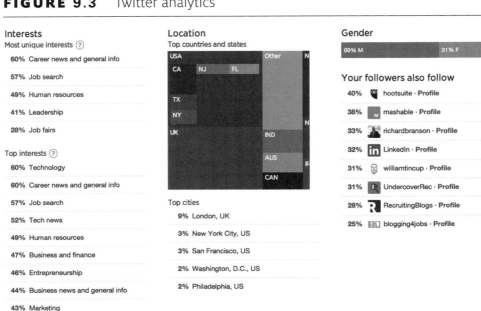

FIGURE 9.4   Twitter engagements

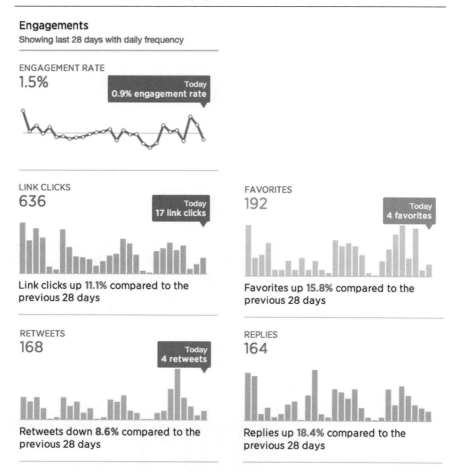

Figure 9.4 shows the different engagements I had during the 28 days, including my engagement rate with my followers, how many times people clicked on the links I shared in my tweets and how many times people retweet, favourite or reply to my tweets.

As you can see, you are now starting to get some interesting data, even at this level. The challenge comes with combining all the social network data into a meaningful dashboard style report each week/month, without adding it all manually. Tools such as Hootsuite and Buffer can provide you with more analytic reports for the different networks that you use via their platforms. As mentioned earlier, every company will have a different set of objectives, requiring slightly different measurement, so my advice would be

FIGURE 9.5   Bio tagcloud

Bio Tagcloud:

#hr acquisition agency author based blogger branding **business** businesses **career** clients **coach** companies company consultancy **consultant** consulting design **development** **digital director** engineering entrepreneur **executive** experience expert **fan** father find firm **follow** food **founder** free global great group **helping human** husband industry interested **job** jobs leading **life** london **love lover** loves **management manager** market **marketing media** mobile music news **online** opinions owner passionate **people professional** professionals **recruiter** recruiters **recruiting** **recruitment** resources **sales search** senior service **services** **social** software solutions sourcing speaker **specialist** staffing strategist strategy **talent** team tech **technology** time training travel **tweets views** web wife **work** working world writer years

to create a bespoke spreadsheet and add in your own metrics each week/month that you wish to track and measure. This only needs to be as complicated as you wish to make it.

If Twitter is a big channel for you, then take a look at SocialBro, as it drills down into every conceivable metric and report you could imagine on Twitter. Many of them are very useful such as the one shown in Figure 9.5. It is a word cloud of the bios of your followers – excellent for showing if you are building an audience (following) that is relevant to your objectives. The words in larger text indicate a bigger density of those words on people's bios. You can see that I am achieving my objective of building a base of followers from recruiting, HR, social media marketing and talent management.

Also, another measure worth considering is the retention of your followers. After all the hard work of acquiring them with your great content, how many do you retain over time? Figure 9.6 shows my retention of my followers (@andyheadworth) over a 12-week period. You can see that I average 100 new followers per week and retain approximately 75 per cent of them.

These may well be useful reports to generate depending on what you are measuring as part of your objectives. A more difficult set of important areas to measure are reach, exposure and influence. These can demonstrate size of audiences and the social media resonance and level of influence you have.

FIGURE 9.6 Follower retention report

Follower Retention Report for @andyheadworth

VIEW Percentage of users ↕

Period	Followers	W 1	W 2	W 3	W 4	W 5	W 6	W 7	W 8	W 9	W 10	W 11	W 12
The week of Jul, 21 2014	102	92%	86%	82%	78%	77%	75%	75%	75%	75%	74%	74%	
The week of Jul, 28 2014	107	94%	85%	81%	79%	77%	77%	74%	72%	70%	69%		
The week of Aug, 04 2014	98	90%	78%	72%	70%	70%	69%	68%	66%	66%			
The week of Aug, 11 2014	128	88%	73%	70%	69%	67%	66%	66%	66%				
The week of Aug, 18 2014	109	96%	87%	84%	84%	84%	84%	83%					
The week of Aug, 25 2014	118	86%	81%	79%	79%	76%	74%						
The week of Sep, 01 2014	101	90%	79%	75%	72%	71%							
The week of Sep, 08 2014	102	87%	77%	74%	70%								
The week of Sep, 15 2014	100	90%	81%	79%									
The week of Sep, 22 2014	110	89%	81%										
The week of Sep, 29 2014	116	95%											

RETENTION   CHURN

Show 12 ↕   weeks ↕   (ROWS)   by 12   weeks ↕   (COLUMNS)

Measuring reach, exposure and influence

There are three areas of social media that are much talked about – reach, exposure and influence – and it is these areas that often cause the most confusion when companies try to use them to establish ROI. Remember first and foremost that we are focused here on using social media for recruiting, not for consumer marketing.

Recruitment metrics can be defined. Website analytics can also be defined, giving you career site metrics such as inbound traffic sources and campaign/link sources. Yet once we start to factor in reach, exposure and influence, attribution and accurate measurement becomes much harder to ascertain.

There are many different interpretations of reach, exposure and influence in the world of social media. Rather than trying to create a complex definition, I have tried to provide a realistic interpretation of each.

Reach

This is the size of the potential audience that could potentially see content that is broadcast by an individual or company. It is made up of the total follower count on each of your social media accounts, including likes on Facebook.

It must be noted that Facebook gives its own analytics around reach, which it defines as 'the number of people who saw your post'. Facebook considers a post to reach someone when it is shown in that person's news feed. They also provide 'total reach', which includes the number of unique people who saw any activity from a page as well as paid versus organic reach.

For example, here is how my reach would be calculated:

LinkedIn connections: 3,500
Twitter: 15,500
Facebook (page likes): 905
Google+ (in circles): 3,700
Recruiting with G+ community: 628
Blog subscribers: 1,200
Newsletter: 9,000
Pinterest: 694
Slideshare: 569

Total reach would be: 35,696 (assuming they are all online at the time and all looked at the content, which never happens!)

Measuring reach is straightforward as it is as simple as calculating the figures each month and watching them grow (hopefully).

Exposure

Exposure is the number of followers each of your followers have. Each time someone shares something on social media, it is shared with their followers and is called an impression. These impressions are included in the exposure of the content shared. This gets a little more interesting and challenging to measure on some platforms, as it again deals with potential rather than confirmed views.

For example, I have 3,500 first-level LinkedIn connections (reach), but these connections have 3.9 million connections (exposure). On Twitter I have 15,500 followers (reach) and they have in excess of 41 million followers (exposure).

There is no way that all my first-level connections and followers are going to share my update and then all their followers and connections reading that same update. However, in the world of social media these are the metrics that are used and this is called *potential exposure*.

As I said at the beginning of this chapter, these are not the sort of metrics that a self-respecting CEO would take seriously. So my advice to you would be to remain very sensible when you start considering using exposure figures in your ROI reporting.

Influence

Rather than trying to explain the complex area of influence, I have turned to Brian Solis to do it for me. Solis is recognized as one of the most prominent thought leaders and authors in new media, and he is a principal at Altimeter Group, a research-based advisory firm. Brian has stripped out anything 'fluffy' and kept his definition very clear and functional: 'Influence is the ability to cause desirable and measurable actions and outcomes.'[1] By including the word 'measurable' in this definition, influence becomes something that is tangible. However, measuring it is a different story.

This is where social media influence starts to enter a nebulous world. There are companies that will tell you they can track and measure influence in social media but, as I have already alluded to, when you have so many 'cross-fertilized' social platforms with multiple layers of relevance (or none at all), gauging or tracking influence is incredibly difficult. Resonance is a little easier to measure or track, as it refers to the activity of others around the content that you produce: do they share, retweet and link to your content in blogs, etc? (You can monitor for this with tools already mentioned earlier in the book.) The more resonance you have, the more potential influence you have.

There are three current tools (Kred, PeerIndex and Klout) that have spent the last few years trying to understand the measurement of influence within social media. They all work to varying degrees, and are certainly worth using as a guide to your social media influence as they provide influence scores.

Ways to use reach, exposure and influence

Here are some ways that you can tie reach and influence into your ROI reporting:

- Track reach on each social network over time to determine where you are seeing the most growth in all your networks.
- When recruiting social media or digitally focused roles that demand experience in those areas, you could use Klout, Kred or PeerIndex as part of the criteria for shortlisting – candidates must have a minimum score.
- Inform future initiatives. Determine what is resonating with your audience by finding what types of content or messaging received the highest exposure. Use that research to perfect future campaigns or content creation.
- Track competitors' exposure to view potential share of voice.
- Compare exposure to mentions to find potential influencers. If the exposure of a specific post was many times higher than its mentions, someone with a large social following is clearly distributing the content. Research the influencer and find ways to work together. They could become a good advocate for your company and your content.
- Combine exposure and reach with engagement metrics to help build a more complete understanding of impact.

Paid social media and ROI

Thus far, everything within this chapter has been related to organic owned and earned social channels – websites, blogs, social networks, brand, etc. In simple terms, you 'own' your own social media entities and earn the right to get the content posted on your pages, shared via different networks and generating your own marketing and PR.

The one area that can produce a defined ROI in social media recruitment is paid-for social media advertising, which I am sure you see every time you use the many social networks you are on: sponsored posts, sponsored updates, Facebook and LinkedIn PPC advertising and Twitter Cards to name a few.

Clever algorithms created by those companies control what you get to see on your social networks such as Facebook, Twitter and LinkedIn. Depending on many factors such as what type of content produces the best engagement (photos, video, text or links), who you are connected with, what you engage with within your network, what you like or retweet and many more actions determines the content you see in your feed. This is obviously a closely guarded secret!

Basically Twitter, Facebook and LinkedIn show you content it wants you to see, not necessarily all the content you want to see. The outcome of these strategies is that they are restricting who sees all the content you post on your social media sites, and making you pay to obtain the reach you once had. To be fair they are also trying to stop 'click bait' posts and low-quality updates from people, but ultimately they are still restricting viewing.

The bottom line is that we are all going to have to start paying for the different types of social media advertising in order to ensure that our important updates and posts reach the desired audiences.

The good news is that you are able to accurately target people via numerous different criteria, so your adverts will only be served to the right audience. Aside from making the adverts appealing, you must send them to a custom landing page (of your creation) with a clear call to action (sign-up page, apply page, follow us, like us, newsletter page, etc). This allows you to determine an accurate ROI for these campaigns.

Example of calculating the ROI of direct sourcing

Here is an example of how to calculate ROI for a company choosing to use direct sourcing to hire some new employees instead of using a recruitment agency.

The objective is to hire 10 new employees using LinkedIn as the social network. There are five different roles (two each of marketing assistant, developer, project manager, community manager and marketing manager), so five job adverts were purchased that ran for 30 days at a cost of £99 each: total £495.

After 30 days, the adverts had received 625 applications in total. As this was for the 10 positions, the cost per job advertised was £49.50 and the cost per application received was 0.80 pence.

After the interview process, all 10 positions were hired. The time and resources accrued by the recruiting team and hiring managers to process the applications, shortlist, interview and offer the 10 candidates was 25 days at a cost in time of £18,750.

Based on previous hires through recruitment agencies the average fees were £4,500 each. Therefore, to hire these 10 roles it would have cost a total of £45,000.

The ROI for using LinkedIn instead is:

$$\text{ROI} = \frac{(\text{return} - \text{investment})}{\text{investment}} \times 100$$

So in this example it would be:

$$\text{ROI} = \frac{45,000 - (18,750 + 495)}{(18,750 + 495)} \times 100 = 134\%$$

Therefore, the ROI for using LinkedIn advertising over recruitment agencies to hire 10 new employees was 134 per cent.

Summary

Establishing a pure social media ROI is possible and one that you may need to demonstrate. Summing up this chapter I would remind you of the following six things in order to ensure you have a chance of doing it successfully:

1 Be clear on your objectives, remembering to align them to business objectives, and know what your targets are going to be.

2 Make sure you are using accurate tracking methods – either existing technologies or using the likes of Hootsuite combined with Google analytics.

3 Make sure you correctly calculate all the time involved in the specific campaigns you run – that is the only way of getting a true ROI.

4 Don't wait until the end of campaigns, and don't be afraid to change poor performing ones several times during a social media campaign. Metrics are all real time, so it should make it easier to do so.

5 Remember that every campaign is different on each social network, due to the different audience types. Patience and persistence is required.

6 Test, test and test again.

Note

1 http://www.briansolis.com/2010/09/exploring-and-defining-influence-a-new-study/.

Social media guidelines

10

There was a time when HR leaders worldwide associated the concept of social media with reduced employee productivity, data security and potential litigation. Social media became the business pariah and access to it was duly banned across many companies. It was frowned upon even to consider social media as a tangible business tool. *Would it surprise you to know that this is still not uncommon?*

It now seems that the business world has finally accepted that social media is here to stay and, whether HR departments agree or disagree with its use, the fact is that existing employees and potential candidates are using social media as part of their everyday working lives. Companies have therefore had to quickly start to understand the dynamics of social media in their workplace. The primary accelerant of this has been the exponential rise in ownership of smartphones such as iPhone, Android, Blackberry and Windows. Social media is so prevalent in the workplace that organizations now need to be aware of what employees say or do on social channels, even if they are not using them directly for work.

In this chapter I explain the need to consider the implications of when things can go wrong on social media from a company perspective. These are not necessarily malicious events, but can be quite innocent mistakes, and often can be down to lack of knowledge or appreciation of what is expected of employees. I look at what a good social media policy should therefore include, and provide you with two excellent examples of social media guidelines that you can use as a starting point to create your own for your company.

A simple and seemingly innocent example of how easy it is to make a mistake on social media involves the current trend for people to take 'selfies' (a picture taken of yourself with your smartphone and posted onto a social network). One of my clients has a very high level of security on-site with a restriction on taking photographs (for very good reasons) in certain parts of the site. Recently some of the new graduate intake decided to take some selfies at their new company. In theory this was okay, as they were standing outside the exclusion zone. They then proudly shared them on Twitter, Facebook and Instagram. What they didn't realize was that in camera shot behind their heads were areas of the site that were 'off limits'. Fortunately this was noticed quickly and all posts were deleted, with a 'don't do that again' message given to the graduates.

While that may sound a dramatic example, just think about your workplace for a minute. What do you have on whiteboards and message boards around your company – talent maps, bids, pitches or client information? I regularly spot things that shouldn't really be shared on social media, in what appear to be innocent selfies taken at work by an employee.

When did you last check to see what has been posted/shared on social networks about your company, brand or people? Do you even check? A good tip would be to use one of the tools from an earlier chapter – Mention.net. Work out all the associated words, abbreviations, anachronisms or keywords and add them to Mention. While this will not be a complete 'catch all', it will help to monitor if there is anything being posted on social media by your employees.

While there will inevitably be some negative issues associated with the use of social media in the workplace there are, however, also many positives to take from it. Social media is an increasingly challenging issue for HR departments due to the growing popularity and ubiquity of social media in our everyday lives. Recruiting departments could, of course, use it to their own advantage should they choose to (within the realms of the law, of course), by using the data posted on the networks to identify, recruit and reference potential new candidates.

However, more and more we are starting to see examples of employees sacked or disciplined for social media misconduct. This could be anything from the 'selfie' photographic example described above, to an employee making disparaging comments. These could be about their employer, colleagues, products, services, competitors, bullying or harassment, misusing confidential information or sharing opinions and comment that (while these may be unrelated to a company's line of business) may reflect badly on their employer's reputation. In fact, one bad instance that goes viral on social media can have long-lasting implications and damage years of branding and marketing. Burger King,[1] Taco Bell[2] and Domino's Pizza[3] have all suffered at the hands of employees sharing unpleasant things they have done while preparing food. Of course this is an area that HR departments have to deal with in increasing numbers – especially as more of the younger generations (who are seemingly always attached to their phones) come into the workplace.

According to the 2013–14 Social Media in the Workplace Around the World global survey carried out by Proskauer Rose LLP, 90 per cent of businesses now use social media for business purposes.[4] Cross-reference this with the 5th annual 2013 Jobvite Social Recruiting Survey,[5] which says that 94 per cent of companies now use social media to support their recruiting, and a Europe-only focused survey by Stepstone, Recruitment via Social Media: Fact or Hype 2013,[6] which says that 69.5 per cent of companies are using social media in the workplace, and it becomes clear that there are social media challenges ahead for HR professionals globally.

Employees seem willing to share information about their company via social media – essential for further building your employment brand – but in a lot of cases they are not sure what they can share in case they break rules or get into trouble. Therefore, it is advisable to put some form of social media guidelines/policy in place to help give your employees some direction, as well as providing protection if employees misuse social media in any way.

If you haven't got a policy or guidelines in place, you are not alone; 20 per cent of companies still don't have one. From surveys, 80 per cent (Social Media in the Workplace around the World, Proskauer Rose LLP) and 81 per cent (Social Media and the Law Survey, ImmediateFuture[7]) of companies say they have them in place.

The problem comes when you decide to create a social media policy for your employees – where do you start? Your location in the world dictates data protection laws, employment legislation and cultural differences, there are different jobs with different responsibilities, and then you have the different variety of social media networks themselves – do you treat them all the same?

The big danger with writing a social media policy (especially where lawyers will be involved) is that it becomes a legal document that is so restrictive and unfriendly that it puts people off wanting to use social media at work. I have seen copies of these types of policies written by top employment law firms, and all they are concerned about is litigation protection (which is what they get paid for, I guess), rather than providing a 'safe' framework to actually encourage employees to share content and interact with people on social media.

There are some companies that have taken simplification of social media policy and guidelines down to one line: don't be stupid, be respectful and apply common sense. While I applaud this approach, it doesn't really provide much guidance or help employees to understand using social media at work.

What should a social media policy cover?

A study carried out by the Institute of Employment Studies (IES) has defined the areas that should be included in a social media policy:[8]

- *Network security*: to avoid viruses, most organizations will have controls on the downloading of software.
- *Acceptable behaviour* and use of:
  - *Internet and e-mails*: if personal use is allowed, state the boundaries.
  - *Smartphones and hand-held computers*: employers need to regularly review and update their policies to cover the new and evolving ways for accessing social media, and to reflect changing employee behaviour and attitudes about their use.
  - *Social networking sites*: remind employees to regularly check the privacy settings on their social networking profiles, as they can change.
    Further, an employer should cross-reference its social media policy to its bullying and harassment policy.

- *Blogging and tweeting*: if an employee is representing the company online, set appropriate rules for what information they may disclose and the range of opinions they may express. Bring to their attention relevant legislation on copyright and public interest disclosure.

● *Data protection and monitoring*: an employer should try to find alternatives to checking staff use of social media, if it can. It needs to justify the use of monitoring, showing that the benefits outweigh any possible adverse impact. An employer should consult with employee representatives or a recognized trade union.

● *Business objectives*: as well as setting clear rules on behaviour, many employers are integrating the use of social media tools into their business strategy. Social networking can be used internally to encourage employee engagement with the organization, and externally to help promote the organization's brand and reputation.

● *Disciplinary procedures*: an employer should try to apply the same standards of conduct in online matters as it would in offline issues. To help an organization respond reasonably, the employer should consider the nature of the comments made and their likely impact on the organization. It would help if the employer gives examples of what might be classed as 'defamation' and the penalties it would impose. Further, the employer should be clear in outlining what is regarded as confidential in the organization.

● *The organization's 'intellectual property'*: this is material that is the result of creativity in the organization – for example, the company logo and brands, a song, copyrights, an invention, patents, designs, etc. The employer should clearly outline what constitutes its intellectual property.

When completed, the social media policy guidelines should then be communicated to all employees through all channels. Some companies I know have added their policy as an addendum to their employment contract, requiring a signature of receipt and understanding. I don't agree with that completely, but I do understand why they might want to do that from a security perspective.

Once the policy is completed and communicated it is very important that it is regularly reviewed throughout the year, to allow for the fast-changing nature of social media.

How to get started on your first social media policy guideline

Fortunately, many companies have been working on their social media policies for a number of years and have produced excellent documents that get the balance right of being great guidelines while at the same time showing common sense. The good news is that (in the spirit of social media) they share them online for other people to learn from and use. Two excellent examples of good social media policy guidelines are from Intel and IBM. They keep them to a one-page document and they are clear and easy to understand.

Intel's social media policy[9]

1 Disclose.
Your honesty – or dishonesty – will be quickly noticed in the social media environment. Please represent Intel ethically and with integrity:

- *Be transparent*: use your real name, identify that you work for Intel and be clear about your role.

- *Be truthful*: if you have a vested interest in something you are discussing, be the first to point it out and be specific about what it is.

- *Be yourself*: stick to your area of expertise; write what you know. If you publish to a website outside Intel, please use a disclaimer something like this: 'The postings on this site are my own and don't necessarily represent Intel's positions, strategies, or opinions.'

- *Be up-to-date*: if you are leaving Intel, please remember to update your employment information on social media sites.

2 Protect.
Make sure that transparency doesn't violate Intel's confidentiality or legal guidelines for commercial speech – or your own privacy. Remember, if you're online, you're on the record – everything on the internet is public and searchable, and what you write is ultimately your responsibility:

- *Don't tell secrets*: never reveal Intel-classified or confidential information. If you're unsure, check with Intel PR or Global Communications Group. Off-limit topics include: litigation, non-published financials and unreleased product info. Also, please respect brand, trademark, copyright, fair use and trade secrets. If it gives you pause... pause rather than publish.

- *Don't slam the competition (or Intel)*: play nice. Anything you publish must be true and not misleading, and all claims must be substantiated and approved. Product benchmarks must be approved for external posting by the appropriate product benchmarking team.

- *Don't overshare*: be careful out there – once you hit 'share' you usually can't get it back. Plus being judicious will help make your content more crisp and audience-relevant.

3 Use common sense.
Perception is reality and in online social networks, the lines between public and private, personal and professional are blurred. By identifying yourself as an Intel employee, you are creating perceptions about your expertise and about Intel:

– *Add value*: there are millions of words out there – make yours helpful and thought-provoking. Remember, it's a conversation, so keep it real. Build community by posting content that invites responses – then stay engaged. You can also broaden the dialogue by citing others who are writing about the same topic and allowing your content to be shared.

– *Keep it cool*: there can be a fine line between healthy debate and incendiary reaction. Try to frame what you write to invite differing points of view without inflaming others. And you don't need to respond to every criticism or barb. Be careful and considerate.

– *Did you screw up?* If you make a mistake, admit it. Be upfront and be quick with your correction. If you're posting to a blog, you may choose to modify an earlier post – just make it clear that you have done so.

IBM's social media guidelines[10]

1 Know and follow IBM's Business Conduct Guidelines.

2 IBMers are personally responsible for the content they publish online, whether in a blog, social computing site or any other form of user-generated media. Be mindful that what you publish will be public for a long time – protect your privacy and take care to understand a site's terms of service.

3 Identify yourself – name and, when relevant, role at IBM – when you discuss IBM-related matters such as IBM products or services. You must make it clear that you are speaking for yourself and not on behalf of IBM.

4 If you publish content online relevant to IBM in your personal capacity it is best to use a disclaimer such as this: 'The postings on this site are my own and don't necessarily represent IBM's positions, strategies or opinions.'

5 Respect copyright, fair use and financial disclosure laws.

6 Don't provide IBM's or a client's, partner's or supplier's confidential or other proprietary information and never discuss IBM business performance or other sensitive matters about business results or plans publicly.

7 Don't cite or reference clients, partners or suppliers on business-related matters without their approval. When you do make a reference, link back to the source and do not publish content that might allow inferences to be drawn which could damage a client relationship with IBM.

8   Respect your audience. Don't use ethnic slurs, discriminatory remarks, personal insults, obscenity, or engage in any similar conduct that would not be appropriate or acceptable in IBM's workplace. You should also show proper consideration for others' privacy.

9   Be aware of your association with IBM in online social networks. If you identify yourself as an IBMer, ensure your profile and related content is consistent with how you wish to present yourself with colleagues and clients.

10   Spirited and passionate discussions and debates are fine, but you should be respectful of others and their opinions. Be the first to correct your own mistakes.

11   Try to add value. Provide worthwhile information and perspective. IBM's brand is best represented by its people and what you publish may reflect on IBM's brand.

12   Don't misuse IBM logos or trademarks and only use them if you have the authority to do so. For example, you shouldn't use IBM in your screen name or other social media ID.

Now that you have read through these two examples, hopefully you can appreciate that your company should have something like these in place to protect both you and your employees when using social media at your company.

Adverse response management on social media

There will be a time when your employees are using social media and they suffer adverse comments or responses. These cannot be ignored and need to be dealt with as soon as possible, as people expect a timely response on social media, and get annoyed when they don't receive one. This is when things can get out of control, as people become progressively more vocal (via social media) and draw more attention to the situation (whether it is right or wrong from your perspective).

The biggest mistake I see companies make on social media within the recruitment and HR industry is to adopt the 9–5, Monday to Friday work hours mentality with regards to social media response management. They will still schedule posts updates, posts and tweets to go out early mornings, evenings and weekends, but won't be there to reply or respond when someone reaches out to them on social media.

When you consider the audience you want to target they are likely to be working, and the best times for them to respond will not be 9–5 Monday to

Friday. Based on that time frame, if someone tries to engage someone at 5.30 pm on a Friday evening, the earliest they will get a response will be 9 am on the following Monday morning – over two days later. That is not acceptable in the fast-paced social media world.

To ensure this doesn't happen to you and your company you need to make sure of the following:

- Select people to manage your social media activities who are comfortable with managing any responses (and being involved in activity) on social media networks mornings, evenings and weekends.
- Provide them with the right tools to do the job – a smartphone and/or tablet or laptop.
- Provide training on response management on negativity.
- Create an escalation tree for any serious issues. This might be as simple as access to a line manager or director.
- Track all the complaints.
- Respond quickly, publicly, on the relevant social network.
- Empathize and acknowledge their complaint/issue, retaining a calm and respective approach when responding.
- If the person is still not satisfied then quickly offer to take it offline and deal with the issue personally.
- Escalate where necessary.
- Don't get drawn into a long back-and-forth dialogue on social media. Make one or two replies maximum.
- Be courteous at all times – remember: this isn't personal.
- There are occasions when I would suggest you don't actually respond. This is when people are deliberately unreasonable and antagonistic, and are usually happy to be spiteful and 'pick a fight'. After an initial acknowledgement and courteous response, don't waste your time with them. 'Starve' them of the attention they are seeking and they will move on to someone else.

The use of social media in recruitment and HR will continue to develop within companies, but will always be a challenge to manage. From my perspective, the companies that embrace social media as a positive and proactive part of recruitment and branding are always going to have more success than those that see it as a reactive problem maker.

Summary

As you have seen in this chapter, using the right social media policy for your company and culture can allow you to take control (as much as you can) of how your employees embrace social media going forward. Now, if you consider that one of the most consistently high sources of hire for companies is employee referrals, and then add the social media empowerment to that, you have a hugely exciting potential candidate network to explore.

With social media being so prevalent and ubiquitous, then, you definitely need to action some of the following items:

- Create some social media guidelines for your employees, which provides them with guidance for their social media activities while working for your company.
- Don't make your guidelines too stringent so that it actually puts people off wanting to participate on social media. You want them to embrace the culture of social media and encourage them to share content with their networks outside the company.
- Remember that social media is on 24/7 and you must have your notifications set up (via e-mail or smartphone) in order to inform you during the evenings and weekends. You may even have to consider social media rotas.

Notes

1 http://www.huffingtonpost.com/2013/08/06/
   burger-king-japan-buns_n_3714602.html.
2 http://www.huffingtonpost.com/2013/06/03/
   taco-bell-worker-licking_n_3377709.html.
3 http://www.huffingtonpost.com/2009/04/14/
   dominos-workers-disgustin_n_186908.html.
4 http://www.proskauer.com/files/uploads/social-media-in-the-workplace-2014.pdf.
5 http://web.jobvite.com/rs/jobvite/images/Jobvite_SocialRecruiting2013.pdf
   IBM social media guidelines.
6 http://www.stepstone.com/default.cfm?pid=/products-and-services/
   recruitment-expertise/download-pdf&file=social_media_report.
7 http://immediatefuture.co.uk/resource/social-media-and-the-law/.
8 The Institute Of Employment Studies http://www.acas.org.uk/index.
   aspx?articleid=3381.
9 Intel social media guidelines http://www.intel.com/content/www/us/en/legal/
   intel-social-media-guidelines.html.
10 http://www.ibm.com/blogs/zz/en/guidelines.html.

Building a business case for social media recruitment

11

Senior executives in any company are busy people responsible for all aspects of managing their business, and recruitment is just one part of it.

While the subject of talent management might be on their agenda, they will be less focused on the tools, methods and technologies such as social media, as these will be left to the HR or recruiting divisions to source, manage and implement. All that is needed most of the time from senior executives is a business case agreed and the budget signed off. When this is a tangible recruitment product, system or service to procure it is a straightforward (albeit sometimes time-consuming) process. ROI is demonstrable and there are usually many direct examples proving this from other companies in similar industries. Senior executives are used to this process and more than likely have previous knowledge and experience of similar products, systems or services. The same cannot be said about social media.

In this chapter I take you through a business-case framework explaining the stages you need to take to create one for your company. There are some steps to take prior to getting started and these will help you when it comes to putting together your business case.

While social media has gone mainstream, there is still a reticence to consider it as an accepted aspect of recruitment and, as such, presenting a business case and subsequently acquiring a budget sign-off is always looked at with more scrutiny. This is not necessarily the fault of the senior executives. HR and recruiting departments have not always been as efficient as they could be in communicating these requests to their senior executives, in the type of business language they understand. For example, you could talk about revenue generation (through better sales hires), cost savings (by initiating direct sourcing and reducing agency spend) and a decreased employee attrition (better-engaged workforce), and so on.

Getting started with your business case

When putting together a business case for using social media for recruiting, you need to be very clear about your objectives. It is very easy when using social media to get carried away with the wrong figures. If you are hoping to make hires through a campaign – one that you are trying to justify with a business case – then don't let your case get bogged down by numbers of Facebook likes, blog subscribers or Twitter followers. The objective should simply be the number of hires over a predefined time frame; that is, after all, what you will be measured against. Of course, you should specify which social media channel they would be expected to come from.

There are a number of key benefits to using social media for recruitment and some, if not all, will find their way into any business case you create for using social media. These benefits are as follows:

1 *Brand awareness*: using social media effectively will lead to more online conversations about your company, your brand and your people. If you are able to reach out to your target audience with social media, it could spread your message to a wider audience faster than traditional methods. Brand awareness will increase whether you are blogging, tweeting, sharing pictures or video, or by having group discussions on LinkedIn. If your content resonates well with your audience, they will further help 'spread the word' and share it with their networks. Before you know it, you will have a marketplace full of advocates talking about your company and your brand.

   It has been proven that the positive power of recommendation has a large influence on decision making (you only have to look at the Amazon review engine for that), and social media influence can have a similar effect on a recruitment brand or candidate acquisition campaign.

2 *Driving traffic to your website/career site*: positive activity (engagement, good content and jobs) on social media networks and online communities generates traffic to your website or career site. Instead of relying on banner advertising, PPC and search engine optimization, it is possible to create engaged and interested candidates (potential employees) from activities and conversations on social media networks. A good example would be writing a post on LinkedIn Publisher that appeals to your target audience. Each time I have done this, the number of people viewing my LinkedIn profile has increased by 300–400 per cent.

3 *Identifying new candidates*: the numbers of people who are now using social networks is mind-blowing and I guarantee that many of them could well be future candidates for your company. Searching for people on these networks is getting easier with the advent of clever tools, such as the people aggregator search products mentioned in previous chapters. This will significantly help your company to

identify potential new candidates without some of the expense of utilizing recruitment agencies every time.

4 *Listening to the marketplace*: monitoring social media helps you to understand your marketplace and industry sectors by keeping you up to date with real-time events. Social media monitoring will help you to learn more about your target audience and clients by tracking potential talent and latest news updates, and watching what they are saying, where they are saying it and why they are saying it. This gives you a chance to engage with them at the right time in order to maximize your chances of a successful dialogue with them.

5 *Search engine optimization*: social media has proven its ability to significantly enhance SEO initiatives. A great deal of social media techniques, including frequent use of common industry terms and keywords, title tags, and links to blogs and other relevant web content, can improve search engine rankings. Due to the popularity of all the main social media networks their content is well indexed and highly ranked by search engines. A web search for companies or people will result in their social media pages and profiles being positioned very highly in the search results. A good test for you is to search for yourself or your company online. Depending on what social media networks you are a member of, your pages/profiles from LinkedIn, Facebook, Twitter, YouTube, Google+, Pinterest or Instagram will likely be on page one of the search results. In many cases for companies, this 'social SEO' ranks higher than their own websites in the search engines.

Overall, social media can be a very cost-effective complementary method for recruiting and could act as a full/partial replacement for traditional recruitment advertising and marketing at a fraction of the cost. Social media works best when it is integrated and coordinated with the rest of your recruitment activities.

How to construct your business case

I have outlined nine steps required to construct a business case for the use of social media in your recruitment strategy, as set out in a one-page framework (Figure 11.1) for easy reference.

1. Define what business problem you are looking to solve

Give a brief description of the problems that the business case is designed to solve. Some examples could be:

● Existing talent attraction methods are failing to deliver both the volume and quality of hire. There is a need for new methods of finding candidates.

FIGURE 11.1   Social media recruiting business case framework

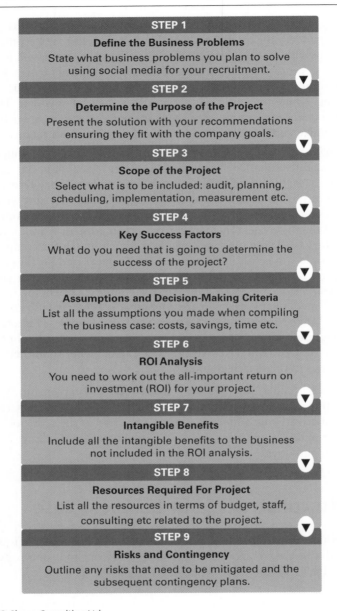

STEP 1

Define the Business Problems

State what business problems you plan to solve using social media for your recruitment.

STEP 2

Determine the Purpose of the Project

Present the solution with your recommendations ensuring they fit with the company goals.

STEP 3

Scope of the Project

Select what is to be included: audit, planning, scheduling, implementation, measurement etc.

STEP 4

Key Success Factors

What do you need that is going to determine the success of the project?

STEP 5

Assumptions and Decision-Making Criteria

List all the assumptions you made when compiling the business case: costs, savings, time etc.

STEP 6

ROI Analysis

You need to work out the all-important return on investment (ROI) for your project.

STEP 7

Intangible Benefits

Include all the intangible benefits to the business not included in the ROI analysis.

STEP 8

Resources Required For Project

List all the resources in terms of budget, staff, consulting etc related to the project.

STEP 9

Risks and Contingency

Outline any risks that need to be mitigated and the subsequent contingency plans.

SOURCE: © Sirona Consulting Ltd

- High numbers of candidates are dropping out during the online recruitment process. There is a need to get candidates who are better engaged and better understand the brand.

- Prospective candidates do not have much awareness of the brand and what the company stands for, and so there is not a high job application rate on the career site. We need to make more candidates aware of the brand and why they should consider working for the company.

- There is currently a static database of candidates that hardly ever gets used and yet there are huge talent shortages in the business. We need to find a way of creating a current talent community from the database.

- Referral candidates have a much better retention rate in the company than applicants via job applications. We need to engage our existing employee base better in order to encourage a better flow of referrals within the company.

2. Overview and project purpose

Present the solution with your recommendations, remembering to include the features and the associated benefits. You will need to obtain buy-in from your project sponsor, so ensure that your project clearly fits with the company's organizational goals. Some examples could be:

- The project is to expand the potential candidate base and identify and engage with new prospective candidates in the industry sector, using the most appropriate and relevant social media networks to do so.

  This means that the existing methods of candidate attraction – recruitment agencies and job boards could be decreased, therefore making cost savings.

- The project is to use engaging content on the social media networks to make more people aware of the brand and show potential candidates what it is like to work for the company. This would increase the number of applications from better-informed individuals entering the recruitment process and making it through to interview.

3. Scope of the project

You need to clearly write what is included in the scope of the project and, equally, what is not. Include any phases and other department/stakeholder involvement, including a timeline for each.

An example would be: this social media recruiting campaign will identify which social networks and techniques are best suited to increase the number of direct hires for the company. The project will be implemented in different phases with training included at each phase.

Phase one – internal and external audit

Review existing recruitment processes and career site functionality for compatibility with social media (ie RSS feed, blog, social sign-in, website analytics, source tracking code, mobile compatibility, etc), competitor activity on the social networks, candidate trend statistics and social network trends.

Phase two – planning and scheduling

Select the chosen social media channels to use, work out a robust content calendar and select contributors, moderators and create social media guidelines. Plan activity levels on the different networks and set provisional engagement targets. Set measurement criteria and measure the success of the project using and ensuring website analytics are ready. Set up keyword alerts to monitor for any brand/people mentions.

Phase three – implementation

Start the project: set up the selected social media channels with appropriately branded profiles and imagery. Commence with activity on the social networks and start posting content and engaging with people.

Phase four – goal indicators

Use activity metrics to assess progress on the project, such as numbers of fans, followers, subscribers, members and people commenting on and sharing the content with their own networks. Adjust activity accordingly if goals are not being met.

Phase five – monitoring

Respond in the social networks where necessary to alerts of mentions of brand and/or keywords (agreed and set up prior to commencement). Continuation of content, activity and user engagement according to the content calendar and activity plan.

Phase six – measurement

Assess the success of the project based on the predetermined criteria of increasing the number of hires, using your web analytics and source tracking.

4. Key success factors

These are important items that you need to include to ensure your project is a success. Examples are:

- We need a budget of XX for consultation and training in order to ensure that employees are adequately trained on the use of the social media platforms.
- Departmental and management buy-in is essential to ensure no hold-ups with the project such as IT blocking access to different social media platforms.
- Executive sponsorship is needed to ensure that the social media recruiting is aligned to employer brand and existing talent management programmes.
- Resources such as time, training time, marketing and IT resources are allocated on an ongoing basis to ensure success of the project.

5. Assumptions and decision-making criteria

List all the assumptions you made when creating the business case, such as costs, savings, volumes, user numbers, resource requirements, time, etc. You should then propose the decision-making criteria that the person reviewing the business case should consider when making a decision. Examples of the types of assumptions made are:

- Potential reach of the information shared on other people's networks will equal the size of their own first- and second-tier network numbers.
- There will be no IT website restrictions for the social media team.
- Two hours per day will be dedicated to social media activity (for purposes of calculating ROI).
- Working hours for the social media team will need to include out of hours.
- Increasing the numbers of fans, likes, followers and subscribers and so on are an indicator of growth.

The decision-making criteria examples could be:

- The successful number of candidates hired through social media sites.
- The cost per hire (it should decrease).
- Time to hire candidates through social media.
- Quality of candidates.
- Levels of candidate engagement.

6. ROI analysis

Work out the all-important ROI for using social media in your recruitment. A simple example for using social media for direct sourcing candidates over a three-month campaign (assuming all hires are then made from candidates sourced on social media) could be:

Recruitment costs: job boards (£4,000); recruitment agencies (£25,000); recruiter's time (£1,000).
Total = £30,000 for hiring six new employees.

Cost of using social media for direct sourcing: LinkedIn recruiter licence (£1,500), social tools (£500), training (£1,000), recruiter's time (£6,000).
Total = £9,000 for hiring six new employees.

The cost saving would be £21,000.
The ROI for the campaign would be 133 per cent.

7. Intangible benefits

Include the intangible benefits that are not included in the ROI analysis. Examples of this are:

- better candidate relationships;
- improved perception of employer brand;
- delayed social media network referrals (could be weeks/months later when people are ready to apply for a job).

8. Resources required for the project

List the required resources in terms of budget, staff, consulting and any other expenditure related to going forward with the business case. Examples of these are:

- budget per projected project costs;
- people resource XX hours per week;
- LinkedIn Recruiter licences;
- training costs;
- management time.

9. Risks and contingency

Outline any risks that need to be mitigated and the subsequent contingency plans. Examples of these are:

- lack of IT support – contingency may be an external IT provider of a social platform such as a blog;
- lack of engagement on social networks – contingency could be encouraging more employees to get involved and/or change the mix of content being posted on the platforms;
- lack of applications on career-site – contingency may be changing the way the jobs are written or advertised, or changing the type of content promoted via the social networks.

Finally (and importantly), include a timed action plan that needs to be carried out with the project. This would include the actions such as budget approval, allocation of people resource and approval of external third parties being integrated into the project.

This is an example template for you to create a business case for using social media for your recruitment. Each one is different, and you will need to develop your own template (you may have one in your business already) and work out the most suitable business case depending on your business needs at that particular time.

CASE STUDY   Example of building a business case

Cigna is a health-care company committed to providing exceptional benefits, expertise and service to its 65 million customers. Known for its dedicated staff, the company strives to find the best possible talent.

Finding the right calibre of qualified candidates in the health-care industry is getting progressively harder. Over the next 15 years to 2030, nearly 50 per cent of experienced health-care professionals are expected to retire. This talent shortage is compounded by additional demand as the baby-boomer generation enters retirement.

Cigna recognized that traditional sources of candidates, such as job boards, had become less effective. It was critical that they find and access a new talent pool, especially in the Chicago area where they had a small presence.

Cigna wanted to strengthen their already well-established employer brand to attract passive candidates in a competitive market. Building out their university recruiting programmes was also essential to fulfil Cigna's long-term hiring needs.

Cigna decided that Facebook was where their target audiences were best placed, so they opted for creating a 'Cigna Careers' Facebook page. This would then make their jobs visible within Facebook and would allow them to be easily shared and accessed by candidates.

They selected the Work4Labs Facebook platform to maximize their chances of success by sharing the content across Twitter and LinkedIn.[1] They also used their advertising to create and promote marketing campaigns to drive candidates to Cigna's career site.

They measured the success of the project on the number of successful placements of health-care professionals in Chicago, cost per application and the improvements in brand awareness and candidate engagement. The project was a big success. They hired 35 professionals in 60 days, with 24 per cent coming directly from job distribution on LinkedIn, Twitter and Facebook. They also saw a dramatic improvement in candidate engagement, and candidate conversions on their career site increased by 50 per cent. This campaign resulted in a cost per applicant of US $28.6, which was far lower than their traditional sources of hire.

Summary

Creating a business case is likely to be something that you do on a regular basis within your company in order to secure budget and resource for projects, recruitment and/or other reasons. Building one for social media should be no different, but be prepared that you may need more evidence and proof of future success. This exact situation happened with a client I was working with, where the CEO wanted almost double the amount of information included in the business case in order to justify a Twitter and Facebook PPC advertising budget for recruitment-focused adverts.

There are some important points in this chapter that are worth a reminder:

- Take the time to work out the objectives and the benefits of the social media recruiting project for which you need to create a business case. The early homework will make the task of creating it much easier and quicker.

- There are many good documented social media recruiting case studies that you can use as part of your business case, but of course they are not always easy to find. There are some great examples included in this book. Another good resource is the business-to-business site **http://www.slideshare.net**, where you will find many other examples.

- Don't discount the intangible benefits – sometimes they have significant benefit for a company even though they may not be as easy to measure.

Note

1 https://www.work4labs.com/learnmore/resources/Cigna%20Case%20 Study%20-%20Work4.pdf.

Future recruitment

12

For many HR professionals social media has become a real thorn in their side. It has caused them many issues in the workplace resulting in an increase in an already heavy workload. It has meant more policies, procedures, guidelines, a need for more training and awareness and (more often than not) a need to urgently review recruiting technologies and processes, and a whole host of other 'people' issues. The key point to remember is that social media adoption and all the associated technologies are ubiquitous and constantly evolving. Therefore, HR and recruiting professionals have no choice but to pay more attention to it in the future.

While social media is impacting HR in different ways, such as access of information, transparency, privacy and compliancy, this chapter focuses on the impact it is having on recruitment, and how social media is making companies change the way they approach recruitment.

To date, the areas where have we seen social media have an effect on recruitment and HR are:

- employer branding;
- communication and messaging;
- candidate identification and sourcing;
- job advertising;
- candidate engagement;
- assessment;
- interviewing;
- information availability;
- data;
- technology and mobile;
- references and background checking;
- transparency;
- the need for speed;
- recruiter skills.

As you can see (and have likely experienced yourself), social media has been a real change agent in our industry over the past two to three years, and it certainly will not be slowing down anytime soon. So how will its impact be felt in HR and recruiting departments over the next few years?

The only guarantee is that future change is certain. To what level and what those changes will be is the million-dollar question, and one that tech companies are constantly striving to solve.

A lesson in future candidate communication from a Roman emperor

Some of the big changes that will have an impact on recruitment in the next few years are not technology-based but people-based. This year alone we have seen the changing behaviours of candidates. Have you noticed how many of the 'sought after' candidates have removed themselves from LinkedIn? They are leaving LinkedIn or downsizing their profiles to such a basic level that they become 'un-searchable' and are moving to other social networks that are more focused on their industry. For example, skilled digital people have moved in large numbers from LinkedIn to sites such as Github and StackOverflow, where there are large specialist communities of their peers.

Also, consider the trend that is occurring in the younger workforce generations (Y and Z) regarding methods of communication. This trend is anecdotal but one that I see regularly across many industries and countries. These candidates want to be communicated with firstly via text-based messaging – e-mails, texts, DMs (Twitter), WhatsApp and WeChat, etc. They don't initially respond well to phone calls and often fail to answer phone calls unless they know or recognize who is calling them on their mobile phones. This is a problem for recruiters. Effectively these candidates have applied their own 'recruiter filter' and will choose who they want to reply to.

This is summed up perfectly by the Roman emperor Cicero back in 80 BC, when he used these words speaking to the senate in Rome:

> If you wish to persuade me, you must think my thoughts, feel my feelings and speak my words.

This can be applied to today's challenge of communicating with candidates. If this trend continues, the effectiveness of recruitment communications to prospective candidates is an area that will have to be improved. To be effective and solicit responses, recruiters will have to engage people in the places that potential candidates frequent and in ways they feel most comfortable. For example, if you are a recruiter in the construction industry, reaching out to construction staff on anything other than a mobile phone will be a waste of time, as they are constantly on site. If you send them links to jobs etc in messages or e-mails, they have to be mobile friendly because they all will be read on a mobile. This may sound obvious, but many companies are still persisting with non-mobile-friendly messaging.

One of the best examples I have seen with regards to 'reaching out' to prospective candidates in a way that would specifically appeal to them is from Matthew Ferree, a technical sourcing recruiter at Amazon in San Francisco Bay area. He recruits software engineers and the like and tailors his messaging to his technical audience. The following is an example of what he sends:

```
cout<<'Hello from Company Name';
Hi [Name]
Please feel free to compile this message.
#include<iostream>
#include<string>
using namespace std;
int main()
{
string yourjob;
cout<< 'Describe your job or company in one word: ';
cin>>yourjob;
if ( yourjob == 'boring' || yourjob == 'lame' || yourjob == 'sucks' ) {
cout<< 'You really need a change. My company is hiring!' <<endl;
} else if ( yourjob != 'challenging' &yourjob != 'exciting' ) {
cout<< 'Why not try something new? We are hiring!' <<endl;
} else {
cout<< 'Thanks for playing!' <<endl; // They'll be back...
}
// TODO: For more info reply to this message or visit
http://companywebsite.com
return 0;
}
```

You may have noticed that this is, in fact, source code. Matthew encourages the developer/engineer to run it through a compiler, which turns the source code into an application. He then asks the candidate to describe their job in one word. If the candidate enters 'boring', 'lame' or 'sucks' the application will tell them that the company is hiring. Or, if the candidate enters any word besides 'boring', 'lame', 'sucks', but not the words 'challenging' or 'exciting' it will encourage them to try something new and let them know the company is hiring. However, if the candidate says their job *is* challenging or exciting, it will thank them for playing and encourage them to visit the website. This is a perfect example of knowing your target candidate audience and, with a little skill, turning your candidate message into a fun approach.

What are you doing to understand the people you are trying to recruit for your company both for now and in the future? My advice is to be brave and take the time to try new methods and techniques – you may hit upon a winning formula that resonates particularly well with your own target audience. Remember the Snapchat example in Dublin in Chapter 2?

Candidate attraction goes mobile

The most common methods for attracting candidates to your company are posting jobs on company career sites, job boards and via aggregators such as Indeed. While most of the job boards now have mobile apps, or at least optimize their websites for mobile and tablet use, the same cannot be said for career sites.

A survey carried out by iMomentus in 2014 on all the Fortune 500 companies found that only 180 had mobile-friendly career sites and, of those, 108 of them do not redirect mobile users to their mobile page, meaning that jobseekers would be unlikely to ever find the mobile career site anyway from their mobile device.[1] Then also consider some jobseeker research carried out by Glassdoor, which found that 68 per cent of jobseekers search for jobs on mobile devices at least once a week.[2]

There is a huge disconnect here. There is no question that the future is mobile and tablet, and yet too many companies are still seemingly ignoring the need to provide a good mobile experience for their prospective candidates. Then factor in that 71 per cent of people use their mobile to access social media, and you realize that if companies are going to successfully embrace social media recruitment, they absolutely must have a mobile strategy in place.[3]

This is not a future change, it should be happening now, in 2015, but it looks like it is going to take longer for companies to adapt. If anyone needs any proof of this then they should look at UPS, who have over the last year made 25,000 hires globally through their mobile and social media channel alone.

CASE STUDY   UPS led the way in mobile recruiting

Back in 2009 the talent acquisition team at UPS started to realize that their traditional recruitment routes of paper, print, cable (TV) and radio were not being as effective as they once were for attracting talent. They recognized that their target audience were already embracing social media, particularly via their mobile phones. To maximize their chances of recruiting this demographic they knew they needed to communicate with them on the platforms they were most comfortable with using – text messaging, Facebook and Twitter – all on their mobile phones. This also meant changing their thinking with their career site, and in conjunction with TMP they created a mobile-friendly website. They also created a new social media UPS 'brand' to differentiate themselves from their UPS consumer side – UPSJobs. This was then used to create branded pages across all the main social media sites.

Matthew Lavery, Director of Talent Acquisition at UPS, says: 'At the time it wasn't proven in the industry that you could use social tools effectively. We needed data to show that social and mobile recruiting could drive strong applicant flow and build the business case for social recruiting.' To ensure they got the required data, UPS used trackable links (auto-generated source codes added to the end of the job links in the ATS) on all their recruitment links, so they could accurately measure the flow of applicants back to the career site. They also tracked and measured other data inside the ATS, including applications, interviews and hires.

To measure the success of the UPSJobs communities they measured activity, growth numbers, levels of engagement and engagement using Facebook Insight Analytics, Twitter Analytics, Google Analytics and Klout scores.

They then embarked on creating a content strategy, focusing around the UPS brand and showing people what UPS is all about – culture, working there and, of course, the other associates. They used three types of content: library content; PR content and press releases. They also empowered new UPS associates, allowing them to create video interviews with senior managers, questioning them about their journeys through UPS from similar starting roles. Other videos and photos were also shared organically from across the company. They proved successful and generated candidate engagement with both the UPS brand and the UPS recruiters themselves.

Lavery anticipated that social recruiting within UPS would require a realistic commitment for two to three years to make it successful. The results have proved that the combination of social media and a mobile-friendly application process worked well for UPS's specific target audience:

- In 2009 (year 1) they hired 19 people.
- In 2010 they hired 955 people.
- In 2011 they hired 2,906 people.
- In 2012 they hired 14,824 (of which 10,000+ were mobile applications).
- In 2013 they made 25,000 hires (of which 20,000+ were mobile applications).

They have now moved their mobile recruitment to the next level with a full mobile-friendly apply process combined with a global UPS job search engine via their mobile platform.

The other significant change that we will see involving candidate attraction is around employer branding. Social media has really accelerated the need (and desire) for companies to be able to show prospective candidates what is behind their brand, and what it would be like to work at their company. This is not something new, but with sites such as Glassdoor expanding globally, and with the viral nature of social media, positivity around a company's visual employment brand presence on sites such as YouTube, Instagram, Pinterest, Vine and Tumblr can have a huge impact on improving recruitment effectiveness.

The Maersk example in Chapter 2 is a perfect example of this. They took to Facebook and used images to create the interest in their brand in order to attract people to their career site, which proved very successful indeed.

If you then consider that all the sites mentioned above (as well as the other main social networks) are all used and viewed extensively on mobile phones and tablets, you then realize that candidate attraction really has gone mobile.

Predictive, automated and algorithmic talent sourcing

You may well believe by now that it is possible to find everyone who has any kind of social media footprint. To a point this is true. Depending on the search method you choose and the time you have, you could in fact find most people across each and all of the social networks.

As we have discussed, people search aggregators, internet browser extensions, data companies with clever algorithms, detailed sourcing techniques and, of course, search engines are all available to recruiters for talent sourcing, mapping and pipelining. So how is this going to change in the future?

The biggest issue is time and convenience. If you have the time, the sourcing skills available and the right budget then getting access to all the talent you need is feasible. But having this data is just the start – what you do with it is where we will see future innovation.

Three words will become more prominent with talent sourcing and recruitment over the next few years – predictive, automated and algorithmic.

Over the next few years, recruitment within companies across the world (including recruitment agencies) is only going to get more challenging as talent shortages continue to cause problems for companies. That said, they are still not utilizing all their 'recruitment assets' to give themselves every opportunity to find the talent they need in order to succeed. The biggest asset that many companies have is the database they have built up from all the adverts they have been systematically placing for years on the job boards. Equally useful are their employees – both current and alumni – as sources of referral leads and talent knowledge. Then you combine these with the people data available on social networks and you have most of the potential talent information that your company could ever need.

The secret to this challenge is how to combine this information and bring it together into a meaningful tool set that recruiters can use to identify, engage with and (ultimately) hire. As of 2015, there are already solutions to these challenges, but they are currently not effectively joined up.

The first area from where a company can produce new talent is their database. Much of the data in current recruitment databases (either ATSs or CRMs) are out of date. Jerome Ternynck, the CEO from Smartrecruiters (one of the modern cloud-based ATS products), sums this up perfectly, by describing most ATSs as 'candidate graveyards' – and he is right.[4] The CVs uploaded into most recruitment systems are quickly out of date and rarely used or ever seen again.

In the future this cannot be allowed to be the case, as talent information is too valuable to waste in this way. One particular company has created a great way of reinvigorating this data and giving it new value – **http:// www.datafreshup.com/**. They have been developing clever data algorithms for interrogating, searching and matching data for a number of years now. Their product takes the people data in your database, combines it with searching over 150 social media sources and, using their proprietary structured data sets and matching algorithms, both enrich the data records and bring them right up to date by adding the current information they find on people. It is very effective indeed and brings your recruitment system or CRM right up to date.

But at the end of the day it is only data – you still have to do something with the information. Why not apply the eiTalent predictive analytics tool to these data records (covered in Chapter 8)? This would then assess your database for potential cultural and skill matches. Add to that some cleverly written automated messaging communications with some artificial intelligence (AI) and then all that 'old data' has started to return some value.

These results could then be used to self-populate segmented talent pipelines, providing real-time reporting on talent shortfalls. The built-in AI would connect with social networks and provide real-time monitoring and alert notifications on your pipelines, to ensure you are fully aware of their status.

For those of you who use LinkedIn Recruiter, some of this is already in place, but of course this includes all the social sites, not just the one network. Then there is the social media talent searching to add in to the mix. We have already covered the people search aggregators, and for many companies these will become as standard a part of their resourcing strategies in the future, as LinkedIn is today.

When you add a new vacancy to your ATS/CRM system it will immediately search all your talent sources in real time, providing you with an accurate talent search prior to you even posting a new vacancy to a job board. If the matches are not suitable then the technology will auto-post out to the most relevant channel for the required talent – job board and/or social media. There are some products that are already doing this, but they are mainly a tick-box approach.

The final part to this is reporting metrics. Comprehensive data information will allow you to make better decisions about your talent needs, recruiting processes and recruiting and hiring teams. The Broadbean product shown in Chapter 8 could well be the benchmark for recruitment reporting suites for the future, but not just restricted to enterprise-level companies.

This technological approach may come across as removing the need for recruiters in the future, but that is not the case. By talking away many of the manual tasks in the recruitment process, it allows recruiters to focus on what they should be doing best – giving them time to hire the best people possible for their companies.

Interviewing via video, mobile and tablet

In 2012 I did not see the value of video interviewing. The technologies were not user friendly (candidate or recruiter) and the results were, at best, not conclusive. Things have changed to the point where, in the future, video-interviewing platforms will become commonplace within recruiting practices for SMEs. They provide a consistent candidate experience, can be used and viewed across desktop and mobile devices and, of course, do not require candidates to spend time and money on attending interviews.

To explain this better, here is the story of how Neil Morrison, Group HR Director, UK and International Companies, at Penguin Random House UK made the decision to trial video interviewing, and why they are rolling it out further across the business.

CASE STUDY   Video interviewing at Penguin Random House UK

On average, Penguin Random House UK receive 300–350 job applications for each of their entry-level jobs. All the applicants have degrees with similar subjects, comparable A-level grades and media work experience. The problem that the recruitment team has is how to differentiate between all these candidates and find the best fit for the company.

The other problem that Morrison highlighted was the tendency of the hiring managers to adopt a 'like for like' approach to making their recruiting decisions, which represented a risk-free approach for them. This approach greatly restricts the flow of new ideas and top talent into the company.

The challenge for Penguin Random House UK was to get the hiring managers to look at a wider range of applicants to ensure they recruited the top talent and diversity. They then acknowledged that they would be asking candidates to make long journeys from around the UK for what could only be a 35-minute interview. This is something they felt was unfair. So they decided to use video interviewing for the first-round interviews.

They selected the Hireview platform for a number of reasons:

- The user interface was dynamic and creative.
- The Hireview team had a high level of passion and energy for what was an evangelical concept at the time.
- The app itself felt like a consumer tech product not a reverse-engineered enterprise product.
- It felt intuitive and natural to use.
- In order that candidates would adopt the concept and actually take the video interviews, Morrison felt that the product needed to be seen to be like a social app that they use every day on their mobile phones.

As soon as the company implemented the Hireview platform, the hiring managers started to enjoy using it. Word spread across the company that it was a good tool, as it saved people's time and was not impacting on them doing their 'day job'. They could control when they reviewed the interviews submitted by the candidates, helping them to fit this in around their workload. They could also pause interviews and return to them if they had urgent interruptions. Some of the hiring managers shortlisted candidates via their iPad on train journeys home; such was the ease of use.

Over a period of two years and 500+ interviews, they have used video interviewing for roles in accounts, HR, marketing, design and sales. They have had 86 per cent of invitees take the video interviews, with a completion rate for roles of 76 per cent. An interesting statistic that came out of the results was that 44 per cent of the candidates who completed their interviews did so at 7 pm.

The best quote comes from one of the hiring managers, who said: 'I would never have hired that person if it wasn't for the video interview process.'

It has proved a very successful tool to shortlist candidates and it has allowed the recruiters to view more potential candidates, as well as saving the company considerable time in the process. Penguin Random House UK is now currently rolling it out across the company worldwide, and starting to use the platform for more senior-level recruitment.

There are many other good video-interviewing platforms to consider besides Hireview, including Sonru, InterviewStream and Launchpad. As with all tech products, each has their own strengths, so make sure that the platform you select reflects the experience you want to give your candidates and your hiring managers.

Recruiting using augmented reality and smartphones

The use of mobile devices in recruitment is now ubiquitous, as demonstrated with the video interviewing example above. Their fast-moving technology continually pushes the boundaries of what can be done with them for recruitment, as is demonstrated by this next example where they 'bring an advert to life' using augmented reality.

CASE STUDY Augmented reality recruiting in New Zealand with ASB Bank

As part of an organization strongly committed to a digital future, the recruiting team at ASB Bank in New Zealand were not satisfied with just using the likes of LinkedIn, Twitter and Facebook from a recruiting perspective. ASB is the challenger brand for corporate and business banking in New Zealand. As such, the team needed to communicate to prospective talent that the bank was doing things differently.

Their objective was to capture the interest of jobseekers in a way they hadn't seen before in New Zealand and, importantly, at the same time make the story shareable across social media to ensure the maximum possible reach. They decided on a 3-D interactive digital recruitment campaign, using an augmented reality app via a smartphone.

To facilitate this project ASB Bank built a microsite and an augmented reality 'Work for ASB' mobile app. When the campaign advertising was viewed through this app, a 3-D augmented reality video of ASB Executive General Manager Corporate, Commercial and Rural, Steve Jurkovich, 'popped out of the page' and started talking to you (as the jobseeker): 'We're constantly redefining banking, through innovation and service. The innovation comes from big investments in technology. The great service comes from big investment in people.'

At the end of the impressive short video (**http://youtu.be/O-YuqOhsF18**), candidates could click on two embedded links on the screen, the first to apply for positions and the second to find out more about ASB's corporate banking business.

Aside from promoting the new recruitment advertising and app via targeted business channels and social media, the ASB acquisitions team created 'Talent Scout' cards. Mark Sumner, Talent Innovation Manager for ASB, explained: 'We knew the type of people that we wished to attract, so we created personalized Talent Scout cards for our corporate banking employees to hand out to this target demographic.'

It seemed that New Zealand embraced this innovative approach for the two-month campaign. There were 4,000+ downloads of the augmented reality app, 200+ job applications and 9 people were hired directly from this campaign. Not bad for an innovative approach to recruiting, not ever seen before in New Zealand. I have left my favourite quote (referring to a newspaper advert during the campaign) from Sumner until last: 'It just caught people's imagination. Someone even tweeted (on Twitter) that their newspaper was talking to them!'

If you haven't seen augmented reality via a smartphone before, enter the YouTube link above into your web browser and take a look – it is very clever.

Recruitment in the future still requires good recruiters

Contrary to what some people in our industry believe, effective recruitment still requires good recruiters to be central in the recruitment strategy. Of course technology can help to enable the recruiting, but when it comes to developing relationships with candidates, engaging hiring managers and managing candidates through counter-offers etc, there is absolutely no substitute for recruiters.

They will, however, have to adapt and change some of the skills they need in order to act as a recruiter in the future. As this book has shown, social media, messaging, technology, candidate empowerment and mobile have made huge impacts on recruitment, so it would be wrong to expect that the skills required to be a good recruiter would not change as a result. These are the areas where skills will need to be improved/changed:

- *Sales and marketing skills.* Recruitment is about sales and marketing – it always has been. First, as a recruiter talking to clients (internal or external) you are selling/marketing yourself and your brand; second, you are then selling/marketing job opportunities to candidates; third, you are marketing your brand, company and yourself via your website, job board advertising and every time you post any update on social media networks.

- *Relationship-building skills.* Recruiters have to be good at developing and managing relationships. These are equally important for clients (internal and external) and with candidates. Recruiters need to develop relationships with candidate networks, focused around the skills and industries that you (as a recruiter) typically recruit for. These quickly become talent pipelines and are extremely important for a recruiter (and the company).

- *Candidate-sourcing skills.* Recruiters need to be able to know how and from where to source the best candidates. Technology can assist them, but they need to know many of the skills shown in Chapter 6 on candidate sourcing. Just searching on LinkedIn won't cut it any more – not when you consider the other options available.

- *Social media skills.* It is a recruiter's responsibility to be where their target candidate audience is, and in many cases that includes social media. But to build a great reputation, and become a recruiter who prospective candidates will engage with, recruiters need to take the time to be active, interesting, to build relationships and develop followings in their specific industries.

- *Contractor management skills.* With the need for skills becoming critical in many areas, companies are turning more and more to hiring contractors, interims and temporary workers. If you are a recruiter who has not before recruited and managed these types of candidates then these skills need to be learned quickly, as they are very different from recruiting permanent candidates.

- *Data analysis skills.* The sheer volume of information now provided to recruiters can be overwhelming. However, this information will be crucial in future decision making, so understanding all the data, what it means and how to manipulate it, is one of the most important new skills a recruiter needs to adopt for the future.

There will no doubt be many other changes within HR and recruitment over the next few years. Social media has certainly been a catalyst for change to date, with technology quickly playing catch-up. But with social media becoming more mainstream, it will be exciting to see where talent innovation will be coming from in the future.

Summary

I chose the topic for the final chapter of this book very deliberately. People in the recruitment and HR industry are always worried about the next new trend, tool or product without properly taking stock of what is already available and proven. The reality is that even in this chapter covering 'future technology' I have focused on things that you as an HR or recruiting professional should be doing right now – mobile and video. They are very much the future of our industry and yet there is still a reticence to use them in recruitment, especially mobile.

I accept that my last example in the book – using augmented reality – may seem a little advanced, but then it has been around for a little while now: I had QR codes on my business cards in 2012. What Penguin Random House, UPS and ASB have shown is that this 'new' tech not only works but is extremely effective in recruitment when combined with technology and social media, and when integrated into their recruitment strategies.

As an HR, recruiting or talent professional reading this book, I hope you are now better placed to understand how your company can use the power of social media as an integrated part of your recruiting strategies. You now have the knowledge to put together and create both a business case for using social media for recruiting, as well as a social media strategy. You have been given some great advice on how to source talent online and via social media from some of the best sourcers in the business. You should now be able to make some informed decisions on which social networks to consider using, and which of the many tools would suit your needs and your budget.

To help you keep things in order the book also includes two great examples for social media guidelines that you can use to both help and protect your employees.

Lastly, I have shown you many great examples of how companies across the world are using social media in different ways to attract and recruit candidates. From simple examples such as the use of BBM in South Africa, to the building of global Facebook communities and the creative uses of Twitter to attract and recruit talent.

I hope the different aspects of this book inspire you to embrace social media and integrate it into your recruitment strategy.

Notes

1 http://imomentous.com/wp-content/uploads/2013/11/Corporate-Mobile-Readiness-Third-Edition.pdf?submissionGuid=1b3e806c-3fa5-467d-87b3-66270ca255f6.

2 http://www.glassdoor.com/blog/infographic-rise-mobile-job-search/.

3 http://blogs.adobe.com/digitalmarketing/mobile/adobe-2013-mobile-consumer-survey-71-of-people-use-mobile-to-access-social-media/.

4 http://sironaconsulting.com/2014/06/09/recruitment-amsterdams-irecruitexpo/.

INDEX

Note: *Italics* indicate a figure or table in the text.